The Truth Through the Truth of Suffering:
Principles and Practical Steps for Suffering Well

Dr. Sue Ellen Nolan MTS, Ed.D

Copyright © 2021 by Dr. Sue Ellen Nolan

All rights reserved. This book and any portion thereof may not be reproduced without the expressed written permission of the publisher except for use of brief quotations in a book review.

ISBN: 9798503968804

Scripture citations, unless otherwise noted, are taken from the *New Revised Standard Version Bible*, copyright © 1999, Division of the Christian Education of the National Council of Churches of Christ in the United State of America. All rights reserved.

Excerpts from the English Translation of the *Catechism of the Catholic Church* for use in the United States of America © 1994, United States Catholic Conference, Inc. -Libreria Editrice Vaticana. All rights reserved.

Cover Image from: Canva & Adobe Spark

Apricus Press
505 Palermo Circle
Fort Myers Beach, FL 33931

This book is lovingly dedicated to my beautiful daughter, Regina, who fought so courageously through this time in her life. She is a superstar and my baby girl.

You are Titanium...

And to my beloved Mother, Ruby "Eleanor" Williams, who gave me the eternal love of God, all through her life, which continues to this day. And who taught me Redemptive Suffering through her glorious example.

To my "Papa" Pope Saint John Paul II
"Be about the business of the Church!"

Acknowledgements:

To my girls, Betsy, Karen, Audrie, and Annette. Your support and love throughout this process has been immeasurable. I love you girls.

To Chad Torgerson, author of *"Waking Up Catholic."* One random, dark day during the Covid pandemic, I clicked on his ad for Spiritual Direction. He encouraged me; on a path he had already traveled. I began to put my workshop on paper and I was on fire again! Thank you for directing me this past year.

To Bill Scheer. Your inspiration, sweet words of revelation from Our Lady, and tears of the Spirit buoyed me up. Anita, I know he is interceding from Heaven. Now is the time!

To Lorie Jo, my BFF. You have been my stress reliever, my sounding board, and my oasis!

To Cathy, for suffering redemptively and consistently, through all this work. Thank you for being there for me in the worst, dark nights.

Thank you to Colleen Snodgrass. You gave my words power and helped me with a temporary charism of writing. Editor from God!

Thank you to Jeffrey Stevens, at *Gospel Grammar* for formatting this baby!

The Truth of Love Through the Truth of Suffering

Table of Contents:

SO, WHAT IS REDEMPTIVE SUFFERING? 5
THE MYSTERY OF SUFFERING 9
THE QUESTION OF WHY 13
THE QUESTION OF EVIL 25
OUR LADY AND SUFFERING: The Mountain Came to Me 41
LESSONS FROM JOB 51
THE CHURCH MEETS US HERE: Our Gospel of Suffering 69
OUR ANTHROPOLOGY: Called Out of Love 83

THE PRINCIPLES:

1. PRINCIPLE ONE: God Took the Greatest Evil and Made it the Greatest Good 111
2. PRINCIPLE TWO: Suffering was Used as the Tool for our Salvation 121
3. PRINCIPLE THREE: There Can Be Joy in Your Personal Gospel of Suffering 127
4. PRINCIPLE FOUR: God is God and We are Not; But When God Shows Up, We Can Do This 135
5. PRINCIPLE FIVE: Suffering Unleashes Love and Evokes Action 149
6. PRINCIPLE SIX: Suffering is a Call to Conversion 159

7. PRINCIPLE SEVEN: Suffering Makes Man Worthy of the Kingdom of God 167
8. PRINCIPLE EIGHT: Redemptive Suffering is a SUPERPOWER! 179

PRACTICAL STEPS TO SUFFERING WELL:
1. GATHER YOUR TWELVE 191
2. DO NOT DESPAIR 197
3. TALK TO YOUR FATHER. 203

THE TRUTH OF LOVE THROUGH THE TRUTH OF SUFFERING: Our Gospel of Suffering 209
EPILOGUE 223
BIBLIOGRAPHY: 224

The Truth of Love Through the Truth of Suffering

Dr. Sue Ellen Nolan

"And we also thank God constantly for this, that when you received the word of God which you heard from us, you accepted it not as the word of men but as what it really is, the word of God, which is at work in you believers."
1 Thessalonians 2:13

"Suffering holds within it a hidden, transformative treasure, an unrecognized gem. Jesus demonstrates how to suffer in how He walks from Gethsemane to Golgotha. Then, in the Word of the Cross, He raises suffering to a Redemptive Superpower. Only if we give assent to uniting our imperfect suffering to Jesus' perfect offering can we open to the superpower Redemptive Suffering contains, and alter the eternal destiny of those towards whom we unleash love, by offering our suffering for them."
Dr Sue Ellen Nolan

"Love is as hard as nails. Love is nails...driven through hands and feet."
C.S. Lewis

So What is Redemptive Suffering?

The ultimate question that each one of us has to ask is: "Is there a Being that exists outside of ourselves, that we call God, and – if that Being exists – will it come into our lives and affect it?" This question is especially appropriate every time we are confronted with suffering, tragedy, or loss in our lives.

We have all heard the simple phrase, "offer it up!" These words seemed benign and especially unexceptional to me until God took me on a journey in discovering the beautiful and unexplored Catholic theology on *suffering redemptively*. Through a series of crises and deep losses, God the Father revealed to me the superpower and potency of redemptive suffering.

So, what is Redemptive Suffering?

Redemptive suffering is a generally misunderstood concept that contains a tremendously valuable, eternity-altering, hidden treasure that has the potential to change everything that you know about suffering. And through the *Word of the Cross,* the word of love that Christ spoke to us when He opened his suffering to humankind, it became a superpower!

In his apostolic letter *Salvifici Doloris, On the Christian Meaning of Human Suffering,* (SD) Pope Saint John Paul II writes to us on the problem concerning the unavoidable widespread human mystery of suffering. For in suffering, he says, "is contained the greatness of a specific mystery." Suffering is set in what is expressed as the "deepest need of the heart," which is to overcome the fear that is presented in suffering, and the "imperative of faith," which means our need for our faith when we suffer. (SD,4)

This formula of the two together leads us to St. Paul's words which Pope Saint John Paul II says seems to be found at the end of the long road that winds through suffering: "Now I rejoice in my sufferings for your sake, and in my flesh, I complete what is lacking in Christ's afflictions for the sake of his body, that is, the church." (Colossians 1:24) (SD, 4)

Christ's suffering is complete and untouchable in the power of the redemption on the Cross of Calvary. There is nothing left to be accomplished in what Christ has done on the Cross. And we cannot, in our humanness, save souls; that is reserved for Jesus Christ alone. This is the objective of redemption, the once-and-for-all acquisition of saving grace and the atonement for all of humankind's sin, and the definitive conquering of death. The unmerited grace that explodes from this action is universally and eternally available for all of us. But we must accept it! This is the subjective redemption that is an inheritance for us. The only action that we have in what Christ has done is to unite our suffering to His.

Redemptive Suffering is available for us to use in a simple prayer of suffering when we unite it with the Cross of Calvary and elevate it to Christ's suffering. That act opens up redemptive suffering to us in God's ultimate plan for the redemption of souls.

A prayer for suffering redemptively:

> "Jesus, I unite my suffering to
> yours on the Cross,
> for the redemption of souls.
> I ask You to use it for [offer intention here]
> Or according to your holy plan."

Dr. Sue Ellen Nolan

"It makes me happy to be suffering for
you now, and in my own body to make up all the
hardships that still have to be undergone
by Christ for the sake of his body, the Church, of
which I was made a servant with the responsibility
towards you that God gave
to me, that of completing God's message,
the message which was a mystery hidden for
generations and centuries and has now
been revealed to his holy people. It was God's
purpose to reveal to them how rich is the
glory of this mystery among the Gentiles; it is
Christ among you, your hope of glory."
Colossians 1:24-27

"When a Man Finds that it is His Destiny to Suffer...His Unique Opportunity Lies in the Way He Bears His Burden"
Viktor E. Frankl

The Mystery of Suffering

Just as Christ's Disciples wrote in their letters of instruction and encouragement to the people of their communities, Pope Saint John Paul II writes to us on an anthropological problem concerning the unavoidable widespread human mystery of suffering.

> ♥ Suffering is a universal theme accompanying man at every point on earth, it co-exists with mankind and therefore demands to be constantly reconsidered. (SD, 2)

Each time we are confronted with suffering – the phone call we get, the knock on the door, the hurt that someone inflicts when they end a relationship, the unfairness in how we are treated in a work situation, and so on – we must reconsider suffering. Often, we will spin into all our human emotions and go into crisis mode. Sometimes we reach out. Sometimes we decide how to cope with the immediate repercussions and often we don't do a good job at it! We look for a salve, an immediate effect that will stop the pain the quickest. We get mad; we might even get mad at God! After the initial response, we come back to ourselves and we look for a step-by-step solution to solving each problem. We dig deep, we gather our support; often we look to see if we have done something wrong somewhere and how the suffering could have been avoided, and we question God's plan for our lives.

> ♥ Suffering seems to be particularly essential to the nature of man. It is as deep as man himself, precisely because it manifests in its own way that depth which is proper to man, and in its own way surpasses it. (SD, 2)

Suffering brings us into ourselves, into the depth of who we are, and we meet the challenges in suffering and ultimately become who we are meant to be. Suffering forces us to go beyond ourselves. We are made for suffering in our Christian anthropology; it is of our essence, not in the way that we desire to fall into suffering or even deserve it, but in the way we are created in the Image and Likeness of God and the way that Christ's life was lived to demonstrate the mystery and success of the glory of suffering well. It is the walk bearing our crosses and arising on the morning of the resurrection. It is the darkness of the road to Golgotha and the light shining from the empty tomb.

The Truth of Love Through the Truth of Suffering

> ♥ Suffering seems to belong to man's transcendence: it is one of those points in which man in a certain sense is destined to go beyond himself, and he is called to this in a mysterious way. (SD, 2)

Ultimately, we are survivors, and we survive by going internally. We search the depth of our souls and pull into our deepest strengths. We discover what we are made of and we can wear our accomplishment like a hidden badge sewn into the ridges of each scar that suffering leaves. We can transcend suffering because Christ elevated His suffering to a mysterious superpower that changed the eternal course of mankind's life for every person and into all of eternity.

> ♥ Suffering is almost inseparable from man's earthly existence. (SD, 3)

The first question I ask at the beginning of my workshop on redemptive suffering is, "Is there anyone here who has not suffered?" It's meant to be funny, though it's not. We all suffer. We will always suffer. Suffering is an inescapable part of our human condition. The act of being born brings us from our warm, safe, sacred, and nurturing environment of the womb into a cold, bright, noisy earthly place. This first act of our birth is our initiation into suffering.

Dr. Sue Ellen Nolan

"We do not want you to be unaware, brothers and sisters, of the afflictions we experienced in Asia; for we were so utterly, unbearably crushed that we despaired of life itself. Indeed, we felt that we had received the sentence of death so that we would not rely on ourselves but on God who raises from the dead. He who rescued us from so deadly a peril will continue to rescue us again."

2 Corinthians 1:8-10

"God had one Son on Earth without sin, but never one without suffering."

St Augustine of Hippo

The Question of WHY

"Why?" It is a question about the cause, the reason, and equally, about the purpose of suffering. In brief, it is a question about the very meaning of the word. The human need for an answer to the question of "Why?" – and the fact that we often receive no satisfactory answer – accompanies suffering and makes suffering precisely 'human." (SD, 9)

In his book, *Arise from Darkness*, Fr. Benedict Groeschel recalls how when he was a young monk he had been driving through a suburban neighborhood at night and came upon a house with an ambulance and police cars in front and with neighbors gathered around. He stopped and went in to see if he could provide spiritual support. He was told that a young couple had lost their firstborn child in the night. As he was brought in the door a young woman was being consoled by relatives. When she saw him enter in his friar robes, she ran to him and grabbed him so hard around the neck that his robes were ripped, while she cried out "Why?!" He knew at that moment that he could not provide an answer, that there might not ever be an answer. And that even as this young mother's life continued, and even if she had more children that question would remain with her forever (pgs. 12 & 13).

Humankind puts the question of "why," Pope Saint John Paul II says, "to God with all the emotion of the heart and with his mind full of dismay and anxiety." That is us, in all our humanness! He continues with this beautiful hope, saying, "...and God expects the question and listens to it." (SD, 10) Our God listens to us. He will not leave us alone in our suffering. He will show up and open our hearts as we seek the meaning to this question of suffering. We will see that God's answer to suffering unfolds in love on the Cross

Both humankind and animals can suffer physically when the body is in pain or hurting, but only humans struggle with seeking a reason for suffering, which can move into moral suffering, described as the "pain of the soul." (SD, 5) This moral suffering is compounded as we struggle with why these things happen to us. We often turn that struggle into blame directed at God. Our beloved Pope Saint John Paul II explains that man puts this blame on God even though suffering often comes from the world, saying, "For, whereas the existence of the world opens as it were the eyes of the human soul to the existence of God. To His wisdom, power, and greatness, evil and suffering seem to obscure this image." (SD, 10)

The Truth of Love Through the Truth of Suffering

The world can reveal to us, in its beauty and grandeur, the existence of God. But suffering can cause us to deny the existence of this same God if we believe He does not provide an answer to the question of "why." In our suffering we sometimes fail to see a solution to the problem of suffering, and proof that He is real and can affect our lives. We live in friendship and harmony with God and His goodness, often until we suffer, when we sever the harmony and order of this relationship.

This story is as old as humankind itself. The Catechism of the Catholic Church (CCC) states:

> The first man was not only created good but was also established in friendship with his Creator and in harmony with himself and with the creation around him, in a state that would be surpassed only by the glory of the new creation in Christ... Our first parents, Adam and Eve, were constituted in an original "state of holiness and justice." This grace of original holiness was 'to share in...divine life.' By the radiance of this grace, all dimensions of man's life were confirmed. As long as he remained in the divine intimacy,

> man would not have to suffer or die. The inner harmony of the human person, the harmony between man and woman, and finally the harmony between the first couple and all creation, comprised the state called 'original justice'. (CCC, 374-376)

There is a potential for this four-part inner harmony in our lives: the harmony of friendship between mankind and God, the harmony within mankind (reason/intellect, between man's soul and body), the harmony between man and woman (persons), and the harmony between mankind and the rest of creation. Through the sin of our original parents, this harmony was lost. God, in His Nature, cannot be the agent of evil. In our suffering, we are often the author of our own evil as we turn from God our Father in sin. Again, a story as old as humankind!

St. Paul wrote eloquently on the mystery of suffering as a two-fold dimension and found his answer to the question of "why?" played out on the Cross of Christ's crucifixion. His answer became revealed in the sharing of the sufferings of Christ because Christ opened His suffering to us, as He shared in all human suffering. In Christ's obedience to His crucifixion, He linked the Cross to love. In turn, Paul offered his sufferings to the Cross which then eventually revealed to him the fullness of the meaning of suffering. When we suffer, the Cross has been opened up to us as well; not only to reveal to us the meaning of our suffering, but to use it, united to Christ's, as Paul demonstrated in love, for the redemption of souls.

Pope Saint John Paul II says that the "Redemption of the world was drawn from the Cross of Christ, and from that, the Cross constantly takes its beginning." (SD, 18) When we suffer with Christ our soul is penetrated with Jesus' presence and the mystery of the meaning of suffering is revealed in love.

The Cross completes the answer to the question of suffering. "...if He loved us in this way, suffering and dying, then with this suffering and death of His, *He lives in the one whom He loved in this way...*" (SD, 20) When we suffer, Christ can live within us because He loved us in this way, from the Cross. Suffering is eternally linked to love.

Our beloved Pope Saint John Paul II writes:

> "but to perceive the true answer to the 'why' of suffering, we must look to the revelation of divine love, the ultimate source of the meaning of everything that exists. Love is also the richest source of the meaning of

suffering, which always remains a mystery: we are conscious of the insufficiency and inadequacy of our explanations." (SD, 13)

Further, suffering is a "mystery, which the individual is unable to penetrate completely by his own intelligence." (SD, 11) When our hearts are cracked open in suffering, we are open to letting Christ be revealed to us in it. This revelation will help us find an answer to "why."

Christ causes us to enter into the mystery and to discover the "why" of suffering, as far as we are capable of grasping the sublimity of divine love. Ultimately, simply – but mysteriously – love becomes the answer to the question of the meaning of suffering.

Pope John Paul II says, "We must above all accept the light of Revelation...insofar as it illuminates this ORDER OF LOVE...as the fullest source to the answer to the question of the meaning of suffering"... (SD, 13)

In other words, when we seek God in suffering, He will show us He is real! And He will reveal to us the mystery of the power that our suffering can have when we unite it to the Cross of Christ.

A few years ago, God chose to demonstrate to me the power of redemptive suffering during a time of

The Truth of Love Through the Truth of Suffering

great suffering in my own life. My mother developed vascular dementia around the age of 75. Many of her eight children took turns with her staying with each one of us, first in Michigan, with my sister Billie Jo (Mom's favorite place) and with Lori Ann, our niece. She would also go to my sister, Brenda and myself, in Florida, and my sister Cheri, in Kentucky. It was a wonderful, terrible time as this disease consumed our mother. When the disease mercilessly took over her mind completely, we moved her back to our childhood town in northern Michigan. My mom had been a nurse and nurse supervisor for thirty years at the hospitals in our hometown. Over the course of those 30 years she supervised many of the nurses coming through the nursing program, taking them under her wing. Many became her friends and would come to our home for Avon parties or Sarah Coventry jewelry parties, which my mom would host. She had a very loving heart, and was excellent at her job. When we brought her home to Michigan, we got her a place in a little facility called "The Annex." Before it became a nursing home, The Annex had been one of the hospitals she had worked at for many years.

Not much about the facility had changed; the furniture and beds were different, of course, but in most respects the small building was completely the same. Mom was so comfortable with her surroundings; she would walk behind the nurse's station and hang out with them. Thanks to her dementia, my beautiful mother thought she was still at work, doing the nursing she loved!

Incredibly, one of the nurses was one of the women that my mom had supervised throughout her life, and had become a good friend of hers. I remembered Margaret from my teenage years. She was about twenty years younger than my mom and simply adored my mother. My mom received the best care in these last years of her life.

Then, in January of 2010, Mom suffered a heart attack and we were called home to be with her. We flew north and we began keeping vigil at her bedside. One evening, after many days by her bedside, waiting for the inevitable, some of us decided to leave for dinner. Our mom had been slowly slipping from us and, at this point, she was unresponsive in her bed. Two of my sisters, both nurses, realized that our mother's breathing was changing, an indication that she was moving into the stage of actively dying and the time had come. Our mother's breathing became labored and she became more restless. We quickly reassembled, with trepidation, knowing we were close to the hour of her death. It was heart-wrenching to sit with her and watch her struggling in breathing and living. My sister Brenda, who had worked as a geriatric and hospice nurse, sat close to her, holding her hand. She wept inconspicuously as our beloved mother's suffering and labored breathing increased. The minutes moved on to hours, and then more hours. My sister was so disturbed by this and said many times that she had never seen this happen this way for so long. It was nearly unbearable for her and for all of us. The shallow breathing and unrest continued. Our mother endured, and we agonized. This continued until early into the new morning. Eventually, sometime after 2 am, our mother took her last breath. Though we were filled with an extraordinary joy in this moment of grace when her eternal love found its source in the next world, we were all distraught with how exceptionally long she had endured this suffering until death finally took her.

Brenda and I headed back to the hotel together after the funeral director had arrived and completed the tasks of the dead. It was somewhere around sunrise. As we settled into our motel room the sky filled with a spectacular winter sunrise, all in shades of orange. My great-niece Emily would later see this from her home nearby and take a picture of it.

We barely spoke, but finally, Brenda said to me, "I don't understand how that could go on for so long! I have never seen that happen before, ever!" In my grief I felt some dawning revelation.

"What is it that mom loves more than anything on this earth?" I asked.

"Us kids," my sister answered.

"How many hours did that go on?"

"About eight hours."

I continued, "I think Mom suffered her last hours, one hour at a time, for each of us eight children…"

I believed my mother had used her suffering redemptively for each of her children in her last hours on this earth. I believed she used the hours as she passed into the next life to suffer for her children's souls. We were able to sit in the peace and profoundness of this. This was my first participation in **Redemptive Suffering 101.**

The Truth of Love Through the Truth of Suffering

Dr. Sue Ellen Nolan

> "We know that all things work together for good for those who love God, who are called according to His purpose."
>
> Romans 8:28

"There is no evil to be faced that Christ does not face with us. There is no enemy that Christ has not already conquered. There is no cross to bear that Christ has not already borne for us, and does not now bear with us.

And on the far side of every cross, we find the newness of life in the Holy Spirit, that new life which will reach its fulfillment in the resurrection. This is our faith. This is our witness before the world."

Pope Saint John Paul II

The Question of Evil

When we suffer, we are drawn to answer the question of why evil exists. When we suffer, we perceive on some level that we have lost a good that we deserve and of which are being deprived. We suffer when we perceive that we "ought to," in the normal order of things, have a share in this good. Therefore, suffering is a double-edged sword. Suffering is always inexplicably attached to the good.

Pope Saint John Paul II defines evil this way: "Man suffers on account of evil, which is a certain lack, limitation, or distortion of the good." (SD, 7) Evil is a difficult concept to define in suffering. We feel that an evil has occurred to us in the loss of something, someone, some circumstance or situation that we considered good for us, that we had a right to. This is moral suffering. There is also physical suffering, which often is the door that leads to moral suffering.

The sin of Adam and Eve was the loss of trust in God and of usurping His place in the universal order. The temptation was to not believe what God had told them about not eating from the Tree of Knowledge of Good and Evil, and to decide for themselves what was

Good and what was Evil. Instead of trusting the almighty God's ability to illuminate this for them in His authority over them, and to know what was best for them, they would do so themselves. This is the sin of us today, the ongoing sin of all of humankind, to eternity! We will decide for ourselves what is Good and what is Evil. We will not trust our Omniscient Creator's moral authority over us. This is the foundation of all disobedience and all sin. Sound familiar?

So, we have the ability to choose evil or good.

Mary Vogrinc, a Catholic mother and speaker, tells a very dramatic story about good and evil and our choices in them. In 2001 she was returning from speaking at a Marian Conference in Pittsburgh, and boarded an American Airlines flight. Her seatmate was a young man who looked very tired, with an overgrowth of stubble on his face, but he seemed cordial and courteous. He helped her get her carry-on bag into the overhead compartment and got her snacks. They began a conversation. He told her he was from Turkey and traveled a lot. As the flight continued, he asked her why she was at a conference. As she explained how she gave speeches and spoke about Jesus and Mary, she noticed a sudden sadness in his beautifully dark, piercing eyes. He then asked her to tell him about Jesus. It was more than asking, it seemed like a demand. She told him what she could about Christ, feeling the intensity of his question. He looked utterly lost to her, like a forlorn child. She randomly asked him what he was running away from; he was taken aback, but the conversation continued. As they disembarked the plane, she wished him a good life and he told her he intended to make some changes in his.

Later, while walking through the airport she noticed him again, this time with a look on his face that frightened her. This time she saw desperation and fear in his eyes as he came urgently in her direction trying to catch up with her. He pursued her through the airport. This scared Mary enough that she thought, "I need to hook up with somebody big." She asked a man nearby where the bus was and when he answered she asked to walk with him. He agreed and they left for the doors out of the airport. As they exited, she lost sight of the Turkish man.

A week later, on September 26th, she was looking through the paper and there was a picture of the man! He was one of the terrorists on the plane that crashed into a field near Pittsburgh, on September 11th 2001. Mary sensed this man was lost and searching for something. Though somewhat caught off guard she attempted to bring Christ to him in those moments with him. Perhaps, if his heart had the

Dr. Sue Ellen Nolan

ability to open to it the sinister mission of his life could have been thwarted.

Many of us remember the sense of doom as the second plane crashed into the North Tower and the comprehension that great evil was at work in this world, right before our very eyes and in real time. Many asked, where was God? When the man who sat next to Mary Vogrinc on that flight home crashed a different plane into the field near Shanksville, Pennsylvania, where was God? As we heard the heart-wrenching stories of loved ones lost and missing, of families shattered and of terror, trauma, and worldwide anguish, people cried, how could a loving God allow such horrors? We all waited in the days after, as the numbers of dead and missing rose, as many of the missing were not found and we realized that they had likely been pulverized in the destruction of the towers that day. We could not fathom such unspeakable evil and pain being permissible to God.

I remember being sure there had to have been 10,000 people, maybe even 20,000 people that had died in those buildings that day. And there must have been 200-plus people on the huge 747s used for this cataclysmic destruction. The actual numbers ultimately shocked me. The planes had crashed into the buildings early in the workday, before the buildings were full to normal capacity. Had they crashed later in the day there would have been thousands more people in the buildings. The planes also had surprisingly low numbers of passengers onboard: one would expect a cross-country flight to have hundreds of passengers, but instead there were only between 70 and 80. And of course there are many stories of people who missed their flights, who were stuck in traffic, who overslept, who switched flights at the last moment. Some survivors recounted tales of improbable escapes, as if they made it out of buildings only through miraculous means. Experiences all too astounding to be pure coincidence, as if perhaps there was a hand in all this in an effort to minimize the havoc evil had wreaked that day.

My good friend Lorie was in New York City, driving by the World Trade Center, early in the morning. Her husband asked her if she had gotten to do all that she wanted on this trip. She mentioned, as they neared the buildings, that she had wanted to go to breakfast at *Windows on the World*, on the top of the World Trade Center. He replied that they could go right then if she wanted to. She hesitated, then decided that they could do it on their next trip since they should head to the airport just to be sure they made their flights. When they landed at Detroit Metro Airport, they saw everyone looking on in terror at the TV screens throughout the terminal at what had happened while they were in flight. That day they were stuck in Detroit for 36 hours, with no cell phone service and no ability to call anyone to tell them they were alive.

In John 16:8, Jesus said that when the Holy Spirit comes, He will convict the world of sin, righteousness, and judgment. The Holy Spirit is made to indwell within us and make us aware of when we turn away from God, our Father. Why does God create evil? He does not! His nature does not allow for Him to create evil, but His permissive will can allow evil to coexist with the good. Often people believe that God cannot be real because of the evil that exists in the world, evils such as global events where many lives of men, women, and little children are lost. How can there be a God who lets this happen? Well, evil has a counterpart in good. Both must coexist. We must have good to compare the loss of it to evil and we must have evil to appreciate the good. This is a double-edged sword. We cannot take full joy in jumping in puddles on a crisp, wet, sun-drenched spring day, when the snow melts and the air smells fresh like new earth, without first enduring the barren, dark, frozen winter.

There is a series of soul-stirring pictures taken by Major Clarence L. Benjamin when he was patrolling in a Jeep on Friday, April the 13th, 1945, near

The Truth of Love Through the Truth of Suffering

Magdeburg, Germany, along with a small task force. They came upon a large group of men, women, and children and discovered they had been packed in boxcars leaving the death camp Bergen-Belsen. Recognizing the Allied troops, they began laughing in joy and near-hysterical relief.

The engineers of the train had been ordered to drive the cars off the end of a bridge into the Elbe River, or blow it all up. The engineers hesitated and stopped the train. When the Allies stumbled upon them, nearly 2,500 people were spared from death.

In some of the greatest incidences of evil in our recent history we see that good is intertwined amongst the evil. The double-edged sword cuts the wound and yet drains out the poison so miraculously that healing can begin. For there to be light, we must have darkness.

Why are some spared death and some are not? Why do some people avoid becoming a victim of a tragedy while some people do not? I remember looking around at my fellow classmates at my high school graduation, and contemplating what lives we would all live and what experiences we would all have. Who would marry first, and have babies, who would become famous or newsworthy, who would travel the world, and even into more morbid thoughts like who would die first, who would lose a child or a spouse, who would get cancer? What hand would we all be dealt, and who was shuffling the cards? Who manifests this plan for we human beings?

When we ponder these stories, we are forced to relinquish our lives to something beyond ourselves. When we realize we have no control, we are forced to believe there is a plan for each life with a determination of their exact time of birth and their exact time of death and the whole dash in the date in between.

We are best off when we turn these thoughts to a real God, a Father, that is the creator of our soul. When we can surrender to this plan – which we realize we can often not affect – we must trust that something or someone is working beyond ourselves. As Pope Saint John Paul II states, "on the far side of every cross," there must be an ultimate plan by an ultimate Creator, and we can rest in this.

According to the *Catechism of the Catholic Church*, freedom is defined as:

> the power, rooted in reason and will, to act or not to act, to do this or that, and so to perform deliberate actions on one's own responsibility. By free will one shapes one's own

life. Human freedom is a force for growth and maturity in truth and goodness; it attains its perfection when directed toward God, our beatitude. (CCC, 1731)

In his early work, *Love and Responsibility,* Bishop Wojtyla, before he became Pope St. John Paul II, demonstrates the need for the proper proportions between negative and positive conceptions of freedom. His analysis of the word "use" points to the conclusion that in the absence of an objective moral order one human being would be free to use the other according to subjective preference (Coughlin, 2003).

The term "individualism," in the Christian sense, values each of us as unrepeatable, unique human beings with a moral worth simply because we are called into existence by the love of our Creator with a purpose and a plan for each of us.

We contain an inherent dignity from being brought into existence through the benevolence of our Creator. The term individualism in the culture today says we don't need anyone, we are self-sufficient. We are here for our own needs, and we have a right to have these needs met, which we can do all on our own! This concept is used to rebel against our desire to be our own god. But this is a counterfeit idea of freedom and the source of Moral Relativism. Peter Kreeft writes, in *A Refutation of Moral Relativism*, "Moral relativism is a philosophy that denies moral absolutes. Moral relativism usually includes three claims: That morality is first of all changeable; secondly, subjective; and third, individual" (pgs. 27 & 28).

What about sin? If there is good and evil, there is good and bad, and we can participate in them. A famous politician made a statement a few years back when asked what sin was. He stated that "sin is being out of alignment with my values" (*National Catholic Register*, 2014).

Well, that makes it easy for us! Good and evil are all relative to what our values are and how they are formed in our personal experience. Therefore, do whatever you want! After all, you can only sin then if it is against your values, right? So sin must not exist! In other words, relativism. "Do whatever you want, as long as it doesn't hurt anybody else." If there is no moral authority to answer to, then, morality is subjective and left to the whims of the moment, without a need for God.

Pope Emeritus Benedict XVI talks of the "Dictatorship of Relativism." He says, "We are moving toward a dictatorship of relativism which does not recognize anything as for certain and which has as its highest goal one's own ego and one's own desires" (Chalk, 2020).

When we lose the order of Natural Law and abandon Absolute Truth, we throw our world into chaos. Our culture destroys the resonating sound of this law in our soul – noise, chaos, distraction, etc. extract us from our being able to hear it. We begin to lose ourselves and our dignity. We move away from being human and more towards being "animal."

The bondage of this culture of relativism leads us to hedonism, tolerance of evil, loss of moral order, and the lack of a need for a God of order or morality. And, ultimately, hopelessness and disregard for life. This is the "Culture of Death," as John Paul II defined (*Evangelium Vitae*, 1995). It leads to bondage instead of freedom, bondage to needs and desires that WE determine, not to a Triune God who knows our best interests; not to a God who loves us beyond our understanding. The cultural definition of freedom is the right to do whatever you want (without moral consequence) but, as Pope Saint John Paul II stated: "Freedom consists not in doing what we like, but in having the right to do what we ought" (Kubasak, 2018).

So then what is sin? Venial sins are transgressions that occur in our daily life, that "allow charity to subsist, even though it offends and wounds." (CCC, 1885). In accordance to the Tradition of the Catholic faith humankind commits mortal sin, encompassing sin against the 10 Commandments, which uses our free will to separate us from our Creator, under these three conditions:

- It is a serious offense against moral law
- We know it is a sin
- We choose to do it anyway

According to the Catechism of the Catholic Church the definition of sin is:

> Sin is an offense against reason, truth, and right conscience; it is a failure in genuine love for God and neighbor caused by a perverse attachment to certain goods. It wounds the nature of man and injures human solidarity. It has been defined as "an utterance, a deed, or a desire contrary to the eternal law. (CCC, 1849)

Sin separates us from God. We move; not God. If there is no moral law or truth that is Absolute, then there is no sin. We can all do whatever we want, which would lead to chaos. We are meant to exercise our free will based on a properly-formed conscience. The jumping off point for such a conscience is laid out clearly in Sacred Scripture in the Ten Commandments.

In our inherited original sin, we are pulled toward evil. Saint Augustine, in *The Confessions,* talks of stealing pears from a neighbor's backyard; he realized he was participating in an evil and of "having no inducement to evil but the evil itself." (pg. 55)

Our nature is that which tempts us towards sin. Augustine continued, "It was foul, and I loved it. I loved my own undoing. I loved my error – not that for which I erred but the error itself" (Ibid. pg. 55*)* This is our fallen nature within us that battles against the good within us. We need the Triune God, the Holy Spirit, and the Sacramental life of the Church for its salve.

A more contemporary reference of our fallen nature can be found in lyrics from a song by a band called The Shins, whom my son, Cody, loved:

> But I learned fast how to keep my head up
>
> 'cause I know there is this side of me
>
> that wants to grab the yoke from the pilot
>
> and just fly the whole mess into the sea.
>
> The Shins, *Young Pilgrims*

Salvation means liberation from sin and evil, and for this reason it is closely bound up with the problem of suffering. Pope Saint John Paul II says:

As a result of Christ's salvific work, man exists on earth with the hope of eternal life and holiness. And even though the victory over sin and death achieved by Christ in his Cross and Resurrection does not abolish temporal suffering from human life, nor free from suffering the whole historical dimension of human existence, it nevertheless throws a new light upon this dimension and upon every suffering: the light of salvation. (SD, 15)

God gave His Son to the world to free us from evil. This love for man, love for the world is salvific love. Pope St. John Paul II continued, "This truth radically changes the picture of man's history and his earthly situation." (SD, 15)

Jesus was given to us to save us from evil, to illuminate our suffering with His salvific love. He came to free us from definitive suffering, from the loss of eternal life. His mission was to conquer sin and death, and the tool He used was His own suffering. In this suffering, He "*blots out* from human history *the dominion of sin*" and in His victory over sin through the resurrection, He "takes away the *dominion of death*" and gives us hope and *"gives man the possibility of living in Sanctifying Grace"* by throwing a new light upon every suffering. "This truth radically changes the picture of man's history and his earthly situation." (SD, 15)

We are born into the time we are meant to be born into. We are born into our families, with all their issues, personally ordained by our Creator to have the issues that we have, to have the struggles that we have, to have the sufferings that we have. He comes into each of these individual stories and desires to meet us there. We are meant to struggle against the evils that slam into us in relationships: our family systems, abuse, addiction, and all the struggles that are custom made for us to encounter. We are meant to seek God in them and let Him meet us there to bring us into the fullness of the being He created us to be: uniquely, unrepeatable, flawed, and fabulous. In the light of the Gospel, love is manifested.

The Word is a **person.**

Dr. Sue Ellen Nolan

"I will put enmity between you [the serpent] and the woman, between your offspring and hers: he will strike your head, and you will strike his heel."

Genesis 3:15

"But especially consider how love draws all the pains, all the torments, travails, sufferings, griefs, wounds, passion, cross and very death of our Redeemer into his most sacred mother's heart. Alas! The same nails that crucified the body of this divine child, also crucified the soul of this all-sweet mother"

St Francis De Sales

The Truth of Love Through the Truth of Suffering

Our Lady and Suffering: The Mountain Came to Me

In 1997 I was just beginning my journey into the Catholic faith, and I was studying all I could about the Catholic faith. During my studies I learned that in June of 1981, Our Lady began to appear to six young teenagers in Medjugorje, on a mountain side, in a small town in Bosnia and Herzegovina. I lived in Northern Ontario, and a parish brought Ivan, one of the visionaries from Medjugorje, there to speak. my friend Terri wanted to go see him, and I agreed to go. The church was very crowded, and it took a while for us to find a place to sit. The first thing I noticed was that, even though the parish was packed full of people, there was a penetrating sense of holiness that I could actually, palpably feel. I hadn't experienced many things like that at that point, and it was the beginning of my initiation into encountering the Mystical contained in the Catholic Church. I might have just been starting my journey to Holy Mother

Church, but I knew I could feel the presence of Holiness.

Ivan told us the story of Medjugorje, and it was so moving and powerful. He told us how every single day Our Lady would appear to him and to a few other visionaries. He called us to mark the time, in our own time zone, when she had appeared to them and set an alarm so that we could be cognizant of Our Lady's presence every day. I set my phone alarm to that time, and ever since that day, straight to the present day, I have paused to bring my children to Our Lady as she continues to appear on this earth.

Ivan said Our Lady told him she comes when her children are most in need, when we are most in trouble, when the world is most in trouble. She asks us to make a decision for God, to not choose the things of the world, and to go into the world with the peace of God, which is in Him alone. He said Our Mother's eyes were filled with love and joy and she had placed us in her heart; and that if we knew how much she loved us we would cry with joy!

I was inspired, and got all the books that I could find on Medjugorje. I spent that cold winter preparing to enter into the Church, reading these books, and taking in the mystery of all this in. I was very moved by Mary, though I knew very little of her at this point. I was amazed at the fact that she was given this singular grace to bring her Son to us, for 2000 years, and to be our last hope as she bears Christ into the world. Even today, through the apparitions, she's bearing Christ into the world. And she's beckoning not to herself, but to Him and telling us again, "Do what he tells you." She is continuing her task of bringing us back to God through prayer, and the conversion of hearts.

A short time later, after I was initiated into the Catholic Church, we moved to South Florida, and a lot of tremendously difficult things happened in my marriage. My kids were around seven and nine. I had a lot of issues in my marriage but tried to live in the Faith through the truth of the Catholic Church and the Sacramental life. The faith was truly holding me up within my marriage.

One day I heard that Ivan, who I had seen in Ontario, and Vicka, another of the Medjugorje visionaries, were going to be at the Basilica of Our Lady Queen of the Universe, in Orlando, on November 7th, 2000 which would be my son's 10th birthday. I decided to take my children on a pilgrimage to the Basilica to see the visionaries so they could hear about the visionaries' experiences.

Dr. Sue Ellen Nolan

As we arrived Father Svetozar Kraljevic, OFM, a priest from St. James in Medjugorje, and Vicka were on the campus praying over individuals. I wanted my son to be blessed on his birthday by Fr. Svet, so we stood in line and he got his blessing, and then Vicka prayed over us. I again felt that presence of Holiness surround me, body and soul.

We went into the church, which was, just like last time, overflowing with people. Since I had little kids with me, the ushers motioned to us to follow them and brought us to a section that had been quartered off for the handicapped, and we were able to sit down. We were tremendously close to the altar and the Visionaries were right in front of us! We knelt down and prayed the rosary out loud and in union. The visionaries, up on the altar, were praying in Croatian and we all prayed in English, of course. As we prayed, that sense of holiness was there in the room. I felt it, and it was very beautiful!

As I was kneeling there, I heard this internal knowledge, this thing that happened that my words cannot convey. I heard Our Lady as she said to me "You're going to have a baby." My initial reaction was very real and very human because I got angry. I felt anger primarily because if she was telling me that I was going to have a baby I did not know how I was supposed to believe this! But the simple words were so profound to me, and I immediately wanted to believe them. But if I believed them and it was not true, I was going to be devastated. After struggling with the emotional ups and downs of infertility, I did not want to believe blindly. It was a very painful thought. But I heard her again as she said, "Trust, trust." It was a very beautiful time and the experience resonated in my soul, but I was not sure what to do about it or how it could have happened to me. It was a very personal, very intimate mystical moment.

During the apparition of Our Lady, as she was appearing to the visionaries there in the Basilica, we were transported to this beautiful place of peace and holiness; and my heart was full of hope and fear.

During the first couple weeks of December I felt this peace inside myself, and I tried to trust in what Our Lady told me, but I also put the thoughts of actually being pregnant out of my mind as it was too much to bear. I told no one what I'd heard that day in Orlando, because it was too personal.

One afternoon a homeschooling friend of mine and I decided to take our kids to see Santa at Publix. I was kind of feeling sick, feeling nauseated, and thinking maybe I had the flu. My brain just could not think beyond that. After we got pictures with Santa, we went back to her house to let the kids play. As I was sitting there it came into my mind that I could be pregnant, and I should tell someone what had happened. But it was so personal! I decided to take the risk and I told my friend. She was a homeschooling Catholic mom, so of course she had a pregnancy test! She got the test and, excited to be in on this secret, told me to take it. I did and it was positive. My brain went numb. I needed more proof so I went to Walgreens and got two more tests. They were positive as well. Eventually the pregnancy was confirmed by my doctor. I realized Our Lady revealed to me something prophetic, and true. God became very real for me!

My life became enveloped in peace. God was real. The world beyond this one had come into my life. My precious baby was growing and my love for God, my Father, was seeping into every aspect of my life for this singular grace He had allowed me. Our Lady had become known to my heart and she was my vigilant Spiritual Mother. She would stay close to me for many years and show herself to me again, in my hour of need. Then, when she had succeeded in her job of bringing me to her Son, she would tenderly draw back. But first, she would stay by my side, literally, for during a time of suffering that would occur in a particular journey in my daughter's life.

My friends were overjoyed, and their faith was made stronger each time I told the story. They felt this baby would be destined for exceptional things. We named our baby girl, born the following July, Regina, after Our Lady, meaning "Queen of Heaven" or "Queen of the Universe." Her existence was told to me in such a mystical way that I knew her life would be powerful. I did not know then, however, how deeply she would suffer and how we would endure tremendous suffering with her.

Saint Simeon prophesied to Mary that "a sword shall pierce through thy own soul also, that the thoughts of many hearts may be revealed." (Luke 2:35) We know from scripture how this played out in Our Lady's life, and yet she still called her only Son out into service at the wedding in Cana. Her consent to suffering never wavered as we saw it played out in the ultimate destiny of Jesus. Her cooperation with His ultimate purpose for the salvation of all of humankind cannot be downplayed. In her youth, she lived out a likely terrifying experience of an Archangel appearing to her. The Archangel Gabriel beckoned her to "not be afraid." (Luke 1:30) Her assent to his offer, as a messenger from God, did not appease any suffering or turmoil, or crisis in her life. She immediately was nearly rejected by the man who she was betrothed to, which would have led to ostracization, humiliation, and an uncertain future. God's continued providence in her betrothed's life, in His ultimate plan, led her into exile in Egypt and the need to escape a murderous, envious ruler. Her young son was then lost from her for three days, and I think anyone who is a mother could empathize with the ice she felt in her heart at that event. Sometime after, St. Joseph dies and she is left a widow.

At the Wedding of Cana, she ushered her Son into His mission in life as she called Him out, knowing that St. Simeon's words would be fulfilled in her heart. The last words of that scripture, "that the thoughts of many hearts may be revealed" (Luke 2:35) call out for the fulfillment of the Messiah. They also spoke deeply to my heart in the suffering that was to follow in Regina's life, that Our Lady was my role model! And my need for God would be profound.

The Truth of Love Through the Truth of Suffering

Dr. Sue Ellen Nolan

> "For I know that my redeemer lives, and at last he will stand upon the earth...."
>
> Job 19:25

> "But is it credible that such extremities of torture should be necessary for us? Well, take your choice, the tortures occur. If they are unnecessary then there is no God or a bad one. If there is a good God, then these tortures are necessary. For not even a moderately good being could possibly inflict or permit them if they weren't. Either way, we're in for it."
>
> CS Lewis

The Truth of Love Through the Truth of Suffering

Lessons from Job

Suffering is a test. In the Book of Job, we find for the first time in Sacred Scripture and God's interaction with humankind that there is a paradigm shift in suffering. The Old Testament God was a God of order, a Lawgiver and Judge, because He is first a Creator who is concerned with the essential good of creation. When humankind consciously and freely violated this good it was a transgression of the law and an offense against the Creator. It was a moral evil (what we now know as a sin) and therefore, was worthy of punishment. Right from the beginning there was an established system – almost like a formula – where good was rewarded and evil punished. This formula is laid out for us: "Thus in the sufferings inflicted by God upon the Chosen People, there is included an invitation of his mercy, which corrects in order to lead to conversion." (SD, 12)

We, in our present life, might know this as a slap upside the head from our Father, God, when our choices turn us toward things that are not good for us or that we know would offend God. The formula begins again: truth and consequence, cause and effect. Suffering is remedial to our faulty behavior and our poor choices. The moral evil of sin is met with punishment. When the Chosen People of God were being led out of bondage, this was the God they encountered most: a just and loving God who answered their prayers and tended to their needs but also a God who set them back on the path as they strayed.

Enter Job, the "just man" who, through no fault of his own, endures an incomprehensible pattern of suffering. He doesn't do anything wrong. Job's friends, convicted in the formula of punishment by God for Job's evildoing, charge him in his suffering to repent of his wickedness and bring God's good compassion back to his life.

In the poetic book of Job, he laments but does not despair as his friends provoke him to admit his wrongdoings and ask for forgiveness. Job's three friends, Eliphaz, Bildad, and Zophar, in fact attempt to vehemently convict him for his sin and error. Job must challenge the assumption of this attestation on the power of his own merits and declare himself an innocent man. Even Job's wife, as she sees her life collapse into grief and suffering, joins in on pronouncing his error and need for repentance. She implores Job to "curse God and die! (Job 2:9) Ultimately this solution sounds better to her in order to relieve the despair she must be undergoing. Job, however, chastises her, saying, "You speak as foolish women do. We accept good things from God; should we not accept evil?" (Job 2:9)

The book of Job reveals a paradigm shift in the concept of suffering. In this sense, it is not about suffering obtained through punishment to restore man to God's order and will. The Book of Job is about an innocent man called into suffering through no fault of his own and who, through his story, demonstrates a more impenetrable mystery on the road of suffering – that is, the question of why do bad things happen to good people. We are not capable of understanding why good people suffer when they've done nothing wrong, without God.

Job is provided a test, to answer a question about why he suffers, as an innocent man; and ultimately, whether he is God or if God is God. Job must, when he is confronted with suffering, stand on not who *he* is but who *God* is to him. Job is provided this test to give evidence of his poverty for God, his need for the Lord. Job demanded the Lord show up, not because he was petulant or cocky, but because Job knew of the power of the Lord to manifest His presence in his life. He knew he needed the Lord right then, and understood that the suffering and evil that befell him was beyond himself so he needed to go beyond himself and to his Lord. Job also knew who the Lord was, that He would continue to be faithful to him in the evil as well as He had been in the good.

There's more to like about Job. Job is a man. We've heard he is a righteous man, but in his suffering, he is a very human man. Job rails against God. That is one short sentence, but the list of synonyms on Google Docs search for "rail" are: "to protest strongly at, make a protest against, fulminate against, rage against, thunder against, declaim against, remonstrate about, expostulate about, make a fuss about, speak out against, express disapproval of, criticize severely."

Job railed against God for chapter after chapter in the Bible. He becomes very human to us in how he rails against God, because we often do the same when we are suffering. Job curses God out, not with curse words, but with expressions where he tells God he is not happy with how things are going. Job questions God even giving him life, he yells at God, he tells God that God has messed up. He gives God the business, just like we would, could, and should. We can use all our humanness in suffering, as well. We are made in our anthropology to have emotions, including anger, and these emotions don't offend God. We have the example of Job who railed against the Lord to show that. Yes, we can rail against Him, in our humanness. We can scream and holler and despise the events that are happening. He has big shoulders and can take it. God, our Father meets us in this.

When we suffer we can call out to our Father, and He will draw close to us in our suffering. We can rail against Him in our human confusion. We can give Him the business! We can ask Him, "What the heck are you doing?!" We can be very human and, it turns out, very much like that righteous guy Job. The Lord will answer us back eventually, though sometimes as an 11th hour God. But He will answer us when we turn to Him. And when He does, we can proclaim the words of Job, "I know that my redeemer lives!" (Job 19:25)

God knows us and how we are made; after all, He made us this way. This goes back on Him, and we just get to be ourselves. We are the ones with the human emotions that go all haywire when we think God has got things wrong. We CAN be angry at God. Let me say that again: we can be angry at God. Anger is a very normal, human response to use when we feel there is little good in our lives. We can yell at God and we can call Him out. We know that behind the anger is hurt, and our Lord will meet us in this, the heart of our suffering, as well. Just as the Lord answered Job when he demanded an audience with Him from the depths of unequivocally suffering, the Lord will answer us when we cry out in anger and suffering. I know this for a fact, because He answered my own Job-like cries of suffering.

In the summer of 2014, at age thirteen, my daughter Regina began to restrict food. She had decided that being a vegan was healthy for her but it was really more of a way of restricting food. She had been bullied in middle school, something we didn't even know until she privately revealed it to her older brother, Cody, later on. What unfolded during her thirteenth year was an obsession with control – the need to control her life, to control her situation, to control her body, to control her unacknowledged pain, her broken family, and her desperation. Regina became furiously combative as her body was unable to contain the intense emotions of her strong, powerful, beautiful personality. She was caught up in adult decisions and events that dramatically changed her young life, the loss of her father through divorce and his moving a thousand miles away back to Canada, the breakup of her family as her sister and brother left home, and the loss of her cherished Grandmother who was a solid source of love her whole life, and she violently rebelled with all of her being. She began to cut herself and threatened suicide. When she could not have what she thought would make her life happy, she struck out desperately against me; and then, one day in early October, she took a handful of over-the-counter sleeping pills. She was taken by ambulance to the hospital, and forced into the children's crisis unit, called Oasis, for a thirty-six-hour psychiatric care evaluation. The psychiatrist there put her on an antidepressant, and our Regina came back to herself for a while. But she continued to restrict her food and self-harm, and rapidly descended into emaciation. One week she self-obsessed over flavored coffee; the next week it was flavored slushy drinks. Her daily diet consisted of little else. If the server got the drink wrong in any way, Regina would meltdown in a tantrum and miss school that day.

As I began to search urgently for some kind of help for my daughter, she spiraled down into a world of secrets and obsession, and fanatical control. Control is related to manipulation and she became a master at it. I could manipulate as well in an attempt to get her to feed her body, to try and pull her back into the life we had had, such as it was. When we first stepped into this world of eating disorders, I had no information regarding what it was and what it wasn't, didn't know what to do or what not to do. There were no resources available to us, nor were there any doctors in our area that took me seriously in these beginning months. Being a single mother, with her father in Canada, our support was limited.

Dr. Sue Ellen Nolan

As our lives took this very difficult, painful, and awful turn, I was becoming more and more spiritually challenged, so I did what I knew I truly needed: I went to find a priest. I needed a priest to help me make sense of what was happening in my daughter's young life. This priest was exactly the person I needed as he affirmed my ragged humanness in my ongoing raging conversation with God. I had been having this conversation with "The Almighty" since Regina's troubles began, and it went something like this: "What the heck is going on here? What the heck are You doing to my daughter? Can You not see this is a little girl? Where is my help in this? Why won't anyone listen to me?" I wanted – needed – answers from God.

The priest I was seeing for spiritual direction, Fr. O'Madagain, talked to me about the parable of the Widow and the Unjust Judge, which had been a recent Gospel reading at Mass. This parable gave me a clear example of where I was with God that day. In the parable, a widow went before a judge to plead her case and demand justice, to demand the "right" order. The woman was angry and demanding, calling the judge out on her case and badgering him to give her justice and what she felt was the right answer. Even though the judge was not a man of God and not a righteous judge, he eventually ruled in her favor simply because the woman relentlessly badgered him.

The Scripture says, "Though I neither fear God nor respect man yet because this widow keeps bothering me, I will give her justice!" (Luke 18:4) The priest told me that God would hear me, even if I relentlessly badgered him and spoke to Him in angry tones. I could be fully human and take all that I felt to God, just like Job. There was freedom in that statement. God became more my Father, where I could be honest in my humanity, and be persistent in my demands of Him. After all, I was fighting for my child, how could I not be demanding? I was going to wait for God to show up!

In November, when Regina's weight was drastically dropping, I introduced our situation to our new family doctor. I explained how I had tried to manipulate her into maintaining her weight by following through on a promise to book a trip for her to go visit her best friend back in Michigan. Regina was desperate to go back there and live her life, even promising that she would not have any problems eating when she was there. In our numerous moves, since the divorce, we had lived in Michigan for the year before her eating disorder manifested. She had been invited to go back for a visit with her friend, Melanie. Once I had our situation explained, I brought Regina in to be seen. In the initial examination, she was weighed but the scale was in kilograms, so I did not know what her weight was exactly. As the doctor examined Regina's 5-foot 5-inch frame, I waited for his concern and a reaction to her obvious issue. He pleasantly acknowledged that she was weighing below an ideal weight and that her trip to Michigan should help her to put on some weight, and that might be a good thing. Then he wished us a good day and dismissed us and walked from the room. I began to formulate a mother's frenzied response in my brain, knowing full well that her weight left her skeletal and that his response to us was not good enough. Regina, of course, was thrilled as he never confronted her self-destruction and gave her an okay to fly to Michigan.

I could not believe the doctor had failed to recognize Regina's obvious emaciation and had given her an okay to fly. She would die if she were left to her own self, I had no doubt. I got her in my convertible and made a broad U-turn from the doctor's office building into the parking lot of the hospital and went directly toward the Emergency entrance. I was determined to find a doctor that would see the reality of what was happening to my daughter and her body, under the control of this demonic eating disorder. She began to yell at me and attempted to jump out of the car as soon as she saw where I was going. She kept saying they were going to put a tube in her and force feed her. Her screams reverberated off the ER entrance's awning, prompting security to come rushing out the door, along with concerned nurses. I told them that my daughter needed to see a doctor, and amazingly, Regina didn't fight the nurses as they took her out of the car and to the nurses' station. Two nurses began to tend to her, one taking her vitals and the other recording them. They were doing their best to talk her down from her hysteria. After a minute I leaned in the door and whispered to the nurse, "What does she weigh?" The nurse had some insight and quietly wrote her weight on a yellow sticky note and handed it to me. 74lbs. Ice ran cold through my veins.

    They walked us to a gurney in the hallway after Regina had changed into a hospital gown, hiding her body defiantly behind the curtain. We waited on the gurney in the hallway for the doctor. Another nurse took blood. The doctor came out to examine her but only superficially, listening to her heart and checking her eyes, etc. He then left. Soon, a man in a white coat came and motioned to me. He explained that they were recommending her to mental health treatment in the children's facility – the same place she had spent three days in when she attempted suicide. I was incredulous. I asked if the doctor had seen her weight, and did he not think she needed to be hospitalized and treated? He explained that she seemed to have mental health issues that needed to be treated in a facility. I told him she had already been at that facility and that there was no treatment there, it was for mental health but not eating disorders. I demanded to see the doctor again. The man disappeared.

A few minutes later he returned and said that the doctor had no further recommendations, but I could take her to the Children's Hospital if I preferred. We continued a heated banter back and forth regarding my daughter's health, but there was no impact. They released her and I took her home. I called her father and updated him. We were helpless at this point, with no medical support.

I spent the night with Regina in my bed. I lay with my hand on her heart, afraid that it would cease beating, while willing my love into her to keep her alive until I could find her help. I slept for a few hours into the early dawn. I woke determined that someone somewhere would do something to save my girl's life.

Suffering teaches us. Through suffering we learn new and better ways to go about life. It is in the form of a test, to direct us toward God and unity with His will, and we learn more about ourselves and about the world around us. Holes are filled in, even ones that lead to better laws that work to protect people more efficiently. Sometimes, families who experience tragedies enact laws that protect others from the carnage that they have experienced in their lives in order to prevent another family from going through what they went through. Suffering allows us to learn what we need to know in our lives and grows us into the person we are intended to be, like gold purified by fire.

St. Alphonsus de Liguori said, "The greatest Glory we can give to God is to do His will in everything" (*Uniformity with God's Will,* 1977). In this we will find our poverty for God. Spiritual poverty is a total dependence on a providential God, and the knowledge that we need Him for every breath, and every meal, and every opportunity. It doesn't mean we stop doing what we need to do, or striving for our goals in life, but this poverty brings us into a surrender to His will for our lives. And we know that we can trust Him in times when we can't see a solution. Our greatest spiritual growth and, ultimately, our happiness comes from uniting our will to His, in what His permissive will ordains for us in our lives. This "conformity" means that we wish to join our will to the will of God. Conformity is consent, which is defined as "The condition of being in harmony or agreement" (*Webster's New World College Dictionary,* 4th ed., 2020). We can go beyond that level of consent to assent. Assent is defined as "to express acceptance of an opinion or proposal" (*Ibid*). Uniformity means assent in that **we want what only God wants and wills for our lives.**

Job desired God's will for his life and assented to it, but still wanted the Lord to show up in it, and provide him with answers. What the Lord did first was reveal Himself to Job. He revealed Himself in His Glory. This became enough, and then it also revealed Job's poverty for the Lord in all things. It was after the grandeur of God was demonstrated that Job fully assented to wanting God's will for his life, no matter the suffering. It was after this revelation of glory and Job's unavoidable assent that he was fully restored. Because Job could answer the question of who God was to him, he then was able to bring his will, though stricken down in suffering, under the uniformity to God's will. Job desired only God's will for His life, in the midst of his suffering. He knew he was a righteous man and therefore he waited on the Lord.

God is not an option, but an absolute necessity. Imagine a life that is free from overwhelming anxiety and fear, full of love and trust in the Creator Who loves us and knows the Good for us for our salvation. We must then accept His will for our lives. And what is God's ultimate will for our lives? Eternity with Him!

How do we know His will? How do we get under God's will? We must unite our will to His in what His permissive will ordains to us. Conformity means that we ask for God's will to be infused in our lives. It means that we can live under His will, giving permission for something to happen or agreement to do something that He wills for us. Uniformity, though, takes the bigger leap. Uniformity to God's will means that **we want only what God wants.** We want His will! We assent in agreement to accepting what He intends for us (de Liguori, 1977). We desire what He wants for us, even in suffering...

Job demanded an appearance from the Lord, and eventually the Lord held true to this faithful man. But he did not take away Job's suffering at that time. Not yet. In the midst of this suffering the Lord showed up and He showed Himself. He "answered Job out of the storm" (during suffering) and told him to "gird up his loins" (translation: toughen up, buttercup, who's got you?). (Job 38:1 & 3) He revealed to Job His Glory and Grandeur. The Lord debriefed Job in a succession of questions about which of the two of them is capable of marvelous things, like founding the earth into the Universe, commanding the morning, walking about at the depths of the bottom of the sea, making the desert bloom with rain, counting the clouds with wisdom, providing for the animals, and controlling Behemoth and Leviathan, to name a few. Obviously, Job is taken to task to understand just Who he was dealing with here. He was being reminded, in a very God-like illustrious way, that God was God and he was not. And, therefore, the mysterious God, powerful and awesome beyond our limited comprehension, had him.

Job understood his poverty for God. And he could rest in it. He could surrender it all again and "know that God could do all things" and that He was in control. The sublimity of his Creator's Divine Love became the answer in his suffering. It was then, after this revelation to Job, that all was restored back to him: "And the Lord blessed the later days of Job more than his earlier ones." (Job 42:12)

Heroic Virtue means trusting in God when you can't see the end in sight and there are no definite answers. Our attitude toward God's will has a direct effect on the quality of our spiritual life. God wills only our good. His will is that we should not lose our souls. When we receive hardships, suffering, evils – as the means that God will grow us in ourselves and to salvation – they become gifts! God wills only our Good, and it happens through these sufferings.

We have the model of St. Joseph for this uniformity with God's will. When Mary was with child, he was troubled and moved to put Mary aside, in a way that would be most protective of her and her reputation.

He would quietly divorce her. But an angel of the Lord appeared to him and told him that God had a plan in this. It took a supernatural event for Joseph to trust in God. He received this tremendous gift because he was called to one of the greatest challenges of all human men. He was to be the stepfather of the redeemer of the world!

St. Joseph's singular calling does not mean we cannot have supernatural events to help us through our suffering; in fact, we absolutely can! When we turn to God He cannot and will not resist us. He will show up for us and show us little whispers of His presence in our life so that we can endure in suffering. These are the events that make God real to us and give us the ability to persevere, no matter what the suffering. We must have eyes and ears for these whispers. We must simply invite God in. He cannot resist us! I invite you to open your tentative heart to this.

Dr. Sue Ellen Nolan

"And not only that but we also boast in our sufferings, knowing that suffering produces endurance, and endurance produces character, and character produces hope, and hope does not disappoint us, because God's love has been poured into our hearts."

Romans 5:3-5

"Simon Cephas answered and said, 'You are the Messiah, the Son of the living God.' Jesus answered and said unto him, 'Blessed are you, Simon, son of Jonah: flesh and blood has not revealed it unto thee, but my Father which is in heaven. And I say unto thee also, that you are Cephas, and on this rock will I build my Church; and the gates of Hades shall not prevail against it."

(Tatian the Syrian — *The Diatessaron*).

The Church Meets Us Here

We can't get by in suffering by doing it on our own. Suffering calls us to learn poverty for God, someone beyond ourselves. If we eventually relinquish ourselves to God, we must connect with a man who lived 2,000 years ago – Jesus Christ. Luckily, He is the ultimate plan of God's salvation for us, and He established a visible and invisible Church here on earth with the Sacraments as a conduit of grace and peace and mercy. From time immemorial, in the Economy of Salvation, our Creator had a plan to save us from ourselves and assist us to heaven with Him.

In Victor Hugo's *Les Misérables*, the character of Bishop Myriel demonstrates to us how the Church can be a vestibule of God's mercy. There have been many film adaptations made of Victor Hugo's 1862 novel *Les Misérables,* but my favorite is from 1978. It stars Richard Jordan as Jean Valjean and Claude Dauphin as Bishop Myriel. In this version we see how an act of mercy from the Bishop demonstrates this very thing to Jean Valjean, an act which breaks open his soul.

Dr. Sue Ellen Nolan

The Bishop's act of mercy brings Valjean's heart back to him and puts him back on course.

Jean Valjean has been sentenced to prison for stealing bread to feed his sister's young children, who are starving. Many injustices occur while he is imprisoned and his time is extended for many years, and during this time his heart turns rock-hard and cold. He emerges later as an altered man, with vengeance consuming his soul and with little prospect of healing, especially once he encounters the stark reality of a life after this prison sentence.

By providence, Jean Valjean knocks on Bishop Myriel's door one night, looking in desperation for food. The housekeeper is frightened and wants to turn him away. The bishop, however, invites him to their table and into their home. Then the bishop gives up his bed to Valjean, a stranger. In the night, Valjean steals the bishop's precious silver and runs off. When he is apprehended in possession of the silver, he is taken to the bishop's home by the *gens d'armes* to confirm the unlikely story he tells that they were given to him as a gift. Incredibly, Bishop Myriel intercedes on Valjean's behalf and substantiates the lie he has told. Additionally, he gives over to Jean Valjean two silver candlesticks, admonishing him that he forgot to take them when he left. Valjean is incredulous at this unwarranted and incredible response of mercy – one that frees him from certain imprisonment once again. Bishop Myriel's mercy has redeemed Jean Valjean's; his iron-hard heart is shredded in this compassion and breaks open from this magnanimous deed.

In the film the bishop then speaks these powerful words to him: "Forget not, never forget that you have promised me to use this silver to become an honest man... Jean Valjean, my brother, you belong no longer to evil, I have bought your soul. And I withdraw from it all black thoughts and I give it to God!"

This act of atonement ambushes Valjean's soul and he combusts in the redemption that is offered. It transforms him and it re-aligns his phenomenology back to the Good. From that point on he looks to do good always, to participate in paying back that precious redemption to all he meets.

Hans Urs von Balthasar calls humankind the "frontier between the world and God," echoing man's inherent dignity in being created in the image and likeness of God. "Man is God's partner, and their reciprocal conversation ends with God Himself becoming man" (*Love Alone is Credible*, 2004, pg. 31). In this conversation we are elevated to the Divine, and our suffering is elevated as well.

Pope Saint John Paul II says:

> In the Paschal Mystery Christ began the union with man in the community of the Church. The mystery of the Church is expressed in this: that already in the act of Baptism, which brings about a configuration with Christ, and then through His Sacrifice – sacramentally through the Eucharist – the Church is continually being built up spiritually as the Body of Christ. In this Body, Christ wishes to be united with every individual, and in a special way, he is united to those who suffer. (SD, 24)

The Church "in Christ is in the nature of a sacrament, a sign and instrument, that is of communion with God" (*Lumen Gentium,* 1964). We have the visible Church to bring us the grace from the invisible Church. We are continually renewed in the Sacramental life, and become more and more Christ-like. The Sacraments and the Church can be the source of enduring strength when we suffer. Through the Sacraments we are united in a real way to Christ in His passion and glorification (St Thomas Aquinas, *Summa Theol.* III q. 62, a. 5 ad. 1). We need to live our faith as the tradition of our life, a real-life relationship with Jesus, in the Sacraments.

Henri de Lubac writes in his book, *The Splendor of the Church,* that:

> ...in the centuries where sacred Tradition had inspired men, there was little or no reflection on the Church, or other mysteries of our Faith, because those people "lived" Tradition. Their lives and their surroundings were saturated with it, and in that sense, not only was reflection not necessary, no one questioned the Tradition. They passed it on without much interference from inside the community. But now, reflection has become necessary, because Tradition itself has become disputed territory (1986, pgs. 15-17).

The Church logically is a focus of John Paul II's writing. Quoted from *Redemptor Hominis,* his first Encyclical, on *Jesus, the Redeemer of Man,* he says "in Christ, every man becomes the way for the Church particularly when suffering enters into life." (RH, 14, 18, 21, 22) When we encounter suffering, each time it must be reconsidered (SD, 2). We must take it out and look at it, sincerely, in an attempt to understand, overcome, deny, or even reject suffering. In that swift, inescapable moment when suffering slams into our present existence, stopping the blood pulsating in our veins and the axis of our universe from going forward, we require something bigger than ourselves to get us through. That "something" is the Church.

In the early years of my life, way before I became Catholic, I remember randomly making decisions and being lost in the world, most especially to myself, and going forward with no direction or real concern. My parents were divorced and I lacked even an earthly father to help guide and direct. There was no Church of my childhood and I had no compass to assist me in life. I was lost and unaware of the degree of the value of a stalwart arrow pointing me in some logical direction. As an adult, I see the value and the need for the Church, even for those who have an earthly father. After my conversion to Catholicism, the Priesthood became my "fathers," and I have consistently sought their counsel in every aspect of my life. Their paternal and supernatural Charism has directed me surely at every point of suffering in my life.

The Church meets humankind on the road when suffering enters our life. Every man is the way for the

Church to meet them in suffering. The foundation of the Catholic Church uses reason and faith for the existence of God which matches our Christian Anthropology in being created in the Image and Likeness of God, *Imago Dei*. We possess a body, mind, and spirit, and are meant to use our whole self – body, mind, and soul – to worship God in the Church. We will go into detail about our Christian Anthropology in the next Chapter.

The mission of the Church is to bring us to God. "The Church's fundamental function in every age and particularly in ours is to direct man's gaze, to point the awareness and experience of the whole of humanity towards the mystery of God." (RH, 10) Humankind's deepest sphere is involved - the sphere of human hearts, consciences, and events.

In his catechetical instructions to the early Christians in the fourth century, St. John Chrysostom, Bishop of Constantinople, beautifully explained:

> There flowed from his side water and blood." Beloved, do not pass over this mystery without thought; it has yet another hidden meaning, which I will explain to you. I said that water and blood symbolized baptism and the holy Eucharist.

> From these two sacraments the Church is born: from baptism, "the cleansing water that gives rebirth and renewal through the Holy Spirit," and from the holy Eucharist. (D' Ambrosio, *Crossroads Initiative*)

This idea is continued in the opening chapters of Lumen Gentium:

> The origin and growth of the Church are symbolized by the blood and water which flowed from the open side of the crucified Jesus (cf. Jn. 19:34), and are foretold in the words of the Lord referring to his death on the cross: "And I, if I be lifted up from the earth, will draw all men to myself." (Jn. 12:32; Gk.) As often as the sacrifice of the cross by which "Christ our Pasch is sacrificed" (1 Cor. 5:7) is celebrated on the altar, the work of our redemption is carried out. Likewise, in the sacrament of the eucharistic bread, the unity of believers, who from one body in Christ (cf. 1 Cor. 10:17), is both expressed and brought about. All men are called to this union with

> Christ, who is the light of the world, from whom we go forth, through whom we live, and towards whom our whole life is directed." (LG, 3)

The blood and water that flowed from Christ's piercing on the cross, is again a method and means of unity with Christ and with the Church. We see the first conversion attributed to the blood and water pouring forth from the body of Christ. St. Longinus is commonly believed to be the centurion who pierced the side of Our Lord while He was hanging on the Cross, he who exclaimed "Indeed, this was the Son of God!" (Mark 15:39) After his conversion at the foot of the cross, Longinus left the army, took instruction from the apostles, and became a monk in Cappadocia. This is the first fruit of the sacrificial Lamb in the birth of the graces that would pour forth from the Church. In myriad ways, Christ established a Church as the conduit of our salvation. The Catechism of the Catholic Church says:

> It was the Son's task to accomplish the Father's plan of salvation in the fullness of time. Its accomplishment was the reason for His being sent. "The Lord Jesus inaugurated his Church by preaching the Good News, that is, the coming of the

> Reign of God, promised over the ages in the scriptures." To fulfill the Father's will, Christ ushered in the Kingdom of heaven on earth. The Church "is the Reign of Christ already present in mystery." (CCC, 763)

My friend Betsy's teenage son, Kent, was diagnosed with a rare cancer. This type of cancer had one form that was common and treatable and one form that was rare and dangerous. Kent had the second one. He bravely endured treatment at the best clinics and eventually went into remission. The Make-a-Wish Foundation provided Kent and his family with a Carnival cruise. The week before they were to leave, Kent was rushed to the ER with severe pain in his lower back. At the hospital, I reminded Betsy that God would not abandon them and that He would show up. Betsy said that she really wanted Kent to receive the Anointing of the Sick, but even as a faithful teenager he was not fully on board. She was scared and shaken and intimidated by this suffering. Kent was being prepped for a biopsy. We were on the Atrium floor at our local Children's Hospital when we noticed our parish priest, Father Hugh, across the balcony floor. Fr. Hugh walked over after he recognized us. We told him that Betsy had hoped her son would receive the

The Truth of Love Through the Truth of Suffering

Sacrament of the Sick, but Kent was irresolute. Fr. Hugh smiled and said. "Oh yeah, no problem! I just went and saw Kent. He was sedated and I gave him the Anointing of the Sick." Fr. Hugh had come to see another parishioner and had recognized Kent's name under Catholic patients. Betsy was pleased and humbled that God had given her this gift, and I never knew if Kent found out he had received the Anointing of the Sick that day while he was under sedation.

The results of Kent's biopsy were bad news. The cancer was back, and throughout his body. The family was still to leave on their week-long Carnival cruise and had to decide at what point to give Kent the bad news in the end deciding to tell him right away. He handled the news with trust in God and they enjoyed their cruise together as a family. After their return, Kent's cancer progressed, though he tried to live as normally as possible.

Prior to his cancer's return, Kent had been working on his Eagle Scout badge. For his service project, he was designing and building a platform for eagles in the woods in southwest Florida. Due to his illness and the breeding cycle of the eagles, his project has been delayed but during the week leading up to his death his fellow Boy Scouts and his father completed his project. In the last days of Kent's life, eagles kept showing up outside the house, despite the fact that

Kent and his family lived in the city. Kent passed away after a courageous battle on November 16th, 2016.

Kent was awarded his Eagle Scout Badge posthumously by his scoutmaster, at his funeral. The Boy Scouts and Kent's teachers from high school and middle school filled the Church to honor this kind, beautiful soul. His cousin gave a powerful Eulogy about the beauty of this young man. The last song for the procession was *On Eagle's Wings*. Some would say that the appearance of eagles outside his home and this choice of song were mere coincidence, but we know otherwise. God is real and the Church meets us in suffering!

The Truth of Love Through the Truth of Suffering

Dr. Sue Ellen Nolan

"Then God said, 'Let us make humankind in our own image, according to our likeness.'"

Genesis 1:26

"The truth is that only in the mystery of the incarnate Word does the mystery of man take on light. For Adam, the first man was a figure of Him who was to come, namely Christ the Lord. Christ, the final Adam, by the revelation of the mystery of the Father and His love, fully reveals man to man himself and makes his supreme calling clear."

Lumen gentium, 22

Our Anthropology

Webster's New World dictionary (2000) defines anthropology as the science of human beings, and especially the study of our "physical and cultural characteristics, distributions, customs, social relationships, etc." (p. 60) The American Anthropological Association (AAA) defines anthropology as the study of humans, past and present, drawing on knowledge from the social and biological sciences as well as the humanities and physical sciences. (www.americananthro.org) Traditionally, archeology discloses the anthropology of humankind in what we do, how we live, our skills, abilities, and intellect which define us externally.

Christian Anthropology, on the other hand, is the study of the entire humankind, mind, body, and spirit as revealed by Christ. It's a study of the dimension of the being of a human person in three parts of this unique whole. And this whole is grounded in the dignity that being the creation of God the Father brings, by being called into relation with Him, to quell the solitude of our soul. Human dignity lies in the call to communion with God; that call lies in the very circumstance of man's origin. Human beings are brought to existence by God's love and preserved by it. Dignity is caught up in acknowledging this truth, in love and devotion to the Creator. (*Gaudium et Spes,* 19) It becomes twofold, in adding God to the equation. Without this truth we are alone.

In *To Know God and the Soul, Essays on the Thought of St. Augustine,* John Teske writes:

> Anthropology was always a twofold question, one about the soul, the other about God. The first makes us know ourselves, the other we know our origin. The former is sweeter to us; the latter more precious. The former makes us worthy of happiness; the latter makes us happy. (Teske, 2008)

In that knowledge of its transcendence and existence, the soul seeks out its Creator and finds its end and its meaning in God. God is all good and man's soul is materially good because it was called into existence by God.

Aquinas said of the soul, "to the extent that it possesses being, it has something good; for, if good is that which all desire, then being itself, must be called good, because all desire to be. As a consequence, then, each thing is good because it possesses actual being." (Aquinas, SCG, III, 7, ad. 3) The good is God, and in possessing the good we are called to the deepest anthropology of our being. Our nature transcends the limits of history and culture.

We get to be human. It is how God created us! He works through this to bring us to Him. He allows us to be us in how we are made. And in essence, the more real human a person is, the more he or she will resemble God. Jesus, after all, is fully human and fully Divine so through this we see the purpose behind the mystery of Christ's dual nature.

The more we understand the nature of human beings, and the more we understand ourselves in this nature, we become the identity that God willed for us and we become more fully ourselves. With deeper awareness, we connect with the soul that inhabits our body, and we "image" God more fully. God is spirit and so are we. Jesus had a body, and so do we.

In Christian Anthropology, we are created body, mind, and spirit. Our soul is an embodied, immortal being, our bodies are "ensouled." We have this internal sense of ourselves, which is our identity, our personality, our temperament, our existence, our being, our thoughts, etc. That's us, and we "image" God in this because He is a spirit as well. Because of this, we tend towards God. We are drawn to God, when we can admit it, because of this anthropology.

There is an image on social media of a rendering of a human cell of DNA, showing all the complexity of our tremendously beautiful design: the colors, the patterns, the details. We often fail to contemplate how amazing we are, created in the Image and Likeness of God, the "*Imago dei.*" We mimic God in that image because we tend toward his goodness. That's why when we do something good, we feel not only like ourselves, but we feel something beyond ourselves. Something within ourselves resonates. We are more ourselves in being more human, consistent in the nature of how God created us, connected to our souls. We feel the "Good" in us, and that good is God. That's how we emulate God. Our physical body might have limitations but our soul is made for eternity. We know we exist for eternity, and this gives us the ability to understand our dignity and value. That makes us want to unite with the "Good", which is God. And so, when the end comes and our body no longer breathes and our cells are no longer living and generating life within it, our soul can end in that Good.

When I was pregnant with my first-born child, after four years of infertility, my husband asked that our children be raised in the Catholic Faith. Since I didn't know much about the Catholic Church, I began to attend Fr. Roy McParland's Wednesday night teachings. As I sat there, full of precious life within me, he opened with these simple words, "God is Love" ... Love overflowed all through me. I felt the presence of God, in love, surrounding me and infilling me. I was moved deeply to the truth that there was eternal life. I was moved to the truth that if there was eternal life then I was responsible for this little baby to be with God in eternal life at the end of his life, by forming him in this truth. It immediately became my responsibility to learn all I could about the Catholic Faith so that I could form him properly in it. This experience of all-consuming love was the beginning of my journey into the Catholic Church.

This profound teaching within our Church Tradition can give meaning to our existence and takes away the despair and hopelessness within our world today. That's part of our total Christian Anthropology and existence. We are called by love into this existence, by our Creator, to be the individual, unique, and unrepeatable person that we are! We are meant to live in this specific era, location, ancestry, and be born into the exact family that we're born into, with its particular issues, problems, and strengths. It is in all this that God calls us to Him, aside from all that might be. He calls us to a relationship with Him where He can be our Father, our Champion, our Healer, and our

Savior. And when we fully comprehend this it becomes our identity.

Next, let us try and understand the mystery of Christ as fully human and fully Divine, called the "Hypostatic Union":

> The Second Person of the Trinity, the Divine Logos, was (and is) God from all eternity. In the Incarnation, he entered space and time as Jesus of Nazareth. While preserving his Divinity whole and intact, he humbled himself by taking on our humanity. This meant creating a human body *and also a human soul* for himself. Jesus wasn't simply a mask the Logos wore, or an *avatar*, or anything of the sort. Rather, the Man Jesus is the Second Person of the Trinity, and vice versa. The Second Person of the Trinity united his human soul perfectly to his Divine Self. In doing so, he bridged the gulf created by sin between God and man. This is one of the reasons that we refer to Jesus by the titles "Son of Man" and "Son of God" without any tension: he's the

> perfect God-Man (*Word on Fire*, 2018).

Christ's place is fixed in humanity. St. Catherine of Siena defined this place as being a chasm, a divide, between Heaven and Earth. The cross of Christ makes it possible for us to leave this world on Earth and exist in the realm of Heaven. Jesus on the Cross is the literal bridge that allows us to intersect this chasm. This bridge is also the bridge of our humanity to the Divine. It elevates us into the glory of God and creates in us the ability to know God and to know ourselves, through our soul. It is the key to our communion with our Creator and the tool for fully comprehending our identity in Christ. We then have the ability, in our body, mind, intellect, and we have grace in our soul, to become all God intended us to be. We are restored to that identity, washed clean from our sins, and filled with Grace.

The Catechism of the Church says eloquently:

> Christ... in the very revelation of the mystery of the Father and of his love, makes man fully manifest to himself and brings to light his exalted vocation. It is in Christ, "the image of the invisible God," that man has been created "in the image

and likeness" of the Creator. It is in Christ, Redeemer and Savior, that the divine image, disfigured in man by the first sin, has been restored to its original beauty and ennobled by the grace of God." (CCC, 1701)

In Christian Anthropology a person is defined in God and through Jesus Christ. They are made in the Image of God (CCC, 1700), but are not gods. We are the *imago dei,* the image of God, different from any other created being and thus possessing an "original solitude," the knowledge that Adam possessed that he was neither God his Creator, nor the creatures he was given dominion over.

Humankind is in His likeness in Jesus Christ as an example of human perfection, and endowed with the ability to be all that they are intended "for faith throws a new light on everything, manifests God's design for humankind's total vocation, and thus directs the mind to solutions which are fully human." (Paul VI, *Gaudium et Spes*, 11) Jesus brought the light of faith to us, in the Church, because He is the light. He illuminates our anthropology and brings a revelation of all we are meant to be in Him and in His light. *Christ is the light of humanity; that light shines out visibly from the Church.* (LG, 1)

The Truth of Love Through the Truth of Suffering

    When my mother was in a nursing home in Northern Michigan, we visited her as often as we could. Since Regina had spent so much of her early childhood in nursing homes she was very comfortable there. Regina was outgoing and extroverted in a very loving way. It just so happened that my sister-in-law's mother, Mrs. Peake, was in the same nursing home. Mrs. Peake was 100 years oldish and for about four years she existed in her bed curled up in a fetal position. She was not interacting with the world. She was not being productive in the sense of the world's ideals. But every single time we went there, my little daughter would want to go see Mrs. Peake. And so, Regina, around age four, would go into her room and she would sit by her bed and she would just chat and hang out with her. Regina could see the value in this little elderly person who could not produce anything, who had no demonstration of what the world would call a productive life. But my daughter saw dignity in her, merely because she existed. She hadn't been tainted by the world to believe that human value lay in producing and not in existing in the Image and Likeness of God. This tiny little elderly woman brought joy to my little girl. She saw the Good in her. She saw God in her, just because she existed! Regina was able to see the Good within us from being made in the Image and Likeness of God. Weakness becomes power when we let God be God. Jesus became weak, small, humble, and dependent: the greatest littleness! Mrs. Peake was the "greatest littleness" in her elderliness and infirmity and Regina was the "greatest littleness" in her youth and compassion.

In 1968, Karol Wojtyla, the Cardinal who would become Pope John Paul II, wrote these words to Henri de Lubac: "The evil of our times consists in the first place in a kind of degradation, indeed in a pulverization, of the fundamental uniqueness of each human person" (*Catholic World Report*, 2019).

Again, the nature of God lives within us and works for a purpose, and coexists with the laws that govern the external universe and the internal soul. This is our Christian Anthropology, the Spirit of God alive within us. But there is a law of order and truth that exists within us, as well, inherited from being created in the Image of God, Who IS all good.

According to the Catholic Encyclopedia on Natural Law (online), "this term is frequently employed as equivalent to the laws of nature, meaning the order which governs the activities of the material universe."

Our God is a God of order. And this is an order that is continually reflected in His creation. This order governs the universe, and includes the earth that His human creation lives upon and, therefore, is bound to participate in. It is determined by God's eternal law and moves us to an end in Him, based on our free-will. Some examples of the laws of the material universe are the Law of Gravity and the Law of Motion.

The Catholic Encyclopedia continues:

> According to St. Thomas, the natural law is "nothing else than the rational creature's participation in the eternal law." (Summa Theologia, I-II.91.2) The eternal law is God's wisdom, inasmuch as it is the directive norm of all movement and action. When God willed to give existence to creatures, He willed to ordain and direct them to an end. In the case of inanimate things, this Divine direction is provided for in the nature which God has given to each; in them determinism reigns. Like all the rest of creation, man is destined by God to an end and receives from Him a direction towards this end. This ordination is of a character in harmony with his free intelligent nature. In virtue of his intelligence and free will, man is master of his conduct.

The laws of nature were created by God and exist within the universe, and the moral laws reside within a human being. Rules of natural law govern every part of our life. There is a Truth that is written in the nature and heart of each individual, to be appropriately expressed through our free will. Natural law equals rational discernment of the natural order as a means of telling good from evil.

George Weigel states in his essays on *The Fragility of Order*:

> Order, it has become clear, is a very fragile thing; and order is especially vulnerable under the cultural conditions of a postmodern world unsure about its grasp on the truth of anything. Order is not self-maintaining. Order is an achievement, and it must be attained, over and again" (*Catholic Digest*, 2019).

This echoes Pope Saint John Paul II's statement in our reconsideration of suffering each time it appears in our life. Each time we suffer we must reconsider it over and over again, and make sense of it, and order it to ourselves, ideally bringing Christ into it.

There is a moral Good that resides within us. We are fully ourselves, who we are meant to be, when we encounter it. This moral good is made of Truth, that is our anthropology! Anything else is a counterfeit. We are created in the image and likeness of God, body, mind/intellect, and spirit. Simply because we exist, we have inherent dignity and value. Our intellect forms our conscience, defined in the Catechism of the Catholic Church as:

> Conscience is a judgment of reason whereby the human person recognizes the moral quality of a concrete act that he is going to perform, is in the process of performing, or has already completed. In all he says and does, man is obliged to follow faithfully what he knows to be just and right. It is by the judgment of his conscience that man perceives and recognizes the prescriptions of the divine law. (CCC, 1778).

The prescriptions of the divine law, or Truth! Jesus said, "For this I have come into the world, to bear witness to the truth. Everyone who is of the truth hears my voice." (John 18:37)

Ideas affect reality. Thoughts that are developed and then spoken or written about affect our culture. Our culture can be formed by the thoughts of individuals that promulgate their beliefs. Thoughts and ideas are shared, read, or seen on movies and T.V. They can be new and novel and form our opinions, which can form our actions.

Ideas can be good or bad but due to our fallen nature, we have a propensity to desire the radical, the scandalous, the progressive, even the dark. We like to be cutting-edge and titillating. It makes us look wise and powerful. Our ideas affect our culture. People agree, and we begin a movement. This movement then forms behavior and soon we have a radical stance on a controversial idea and we are trend-setters, admired, and worshiped. Ideas grow power.

How do we know which ideas are "good" and which ideas are "bad?" Instinctively within us, we all recognize a tendency for the "good." The good is contained within our human nature. We tend towards the good. Even a thief doesn't want to be stolen from. We have a core center of natural good within us; it is a law written upon our hearts. This core center of knowing good comes from our Christian Anthropology of knowing we are created in the Image and Likeness of God. We "image" God because He is by definition all "Good." We tend toward this "good." When we are motivated to do good it is from within our nature that is made in the Image of God. We know this Good when it echoes in our soul.

My favorite example of how humans are motivated to do good and feel the "Good" is from when we traveled to Daytona Beach for a cheer competition with my daughter, Regina and her friend, Meghan. The girls needed hairspray, which is a staple for cheer, so one morning we walked to Walgreens with a couple of the moms and a group of the girls. As we made our way back to our ocean-side hotel we noticed this elderly couple on the side of the building with a shopping cart. What I didn't notice, but the girls did, was that this little, grey-haired, elderly couple was gathering food out of the dumpster. The girls were shocked and deeply moved. They immediately asked if they could get food from our continental breakfast bar and give it to this elderly couple, and we said yes. The girls gathered muffins and fruit and juices and hurriedly brought the offerings out to this hungry couple. The expression on the girl's faces was unforgettable, and one of complete purpose in feeding the old people. These girls were triumphant in their simple success. It was not pride on their faces; it was goodness. They felt it in their souls and it radiated outward. To this day Regina could not tell me where they placed in that competition but she will never forget that feeling in the moment of participating in the Good of God.

There was a video circulating of a little boy of about six years old trying to break a board with his foot in a martial arts class. His classmates were sitting around him watching his failed attempts. He tried repeatedly to break the board, but time and time again he could not. The determination on his little face fell out of his eyes in tears. Yet, none of his very young teammates or competitors ridiculed him or said mean things to him. As he cried in frustration, his instructor patiently coached and encouraged him. He demonstrated to him the proper way to break the board. He endures without breaking the board. But finally, the board breaks! In the exaltation, he is nearly knocked over by the kids rushing him in elation for his perseverance and success. Do you FEEL the Good? This Good is innate within us. We recognize it when we experience it.

Pope Saint John Paul II sums this up:

> The dignity of the human person is a transcendent value, always recognized as such by those who sincerely search for the truth. Indeed, the whole of human history should be interpreted in the light of

> this certainty. Every person, created in the image and likeness of God (cf. Gn 1:26 28), is therefore radically oriented towards the Creator, and is constantly in relationship with those possessed of the same dignity. To promote the good of the individual is thus to serve the common good, which is that point where rights and duties converge and reinforce one another (Pope John Paul II, 1999).

There is a natural order that orders our anthropology, our nature, our souls, and our egos. When we know our poverty for God, that He is our Creator and that He loved us into existence and holds us there, we can be fully ourselves. We can know that we need Him beyond and above all earthly things. When we know this, we can "rest" in the natural order that God, Himself has created. Truth is written in our Christian Anthropology! When we lose the sense of this order, we lose ourselves.

During the 17th and 18th centuries we saw the rise of the Age of Enlightenment, a period when philosophical ideas formed the culture and led to a movement that began an annihilation of God. During this period, ideas concerning God, reason, nature, and humanity were synthesized into a worldview that gained wide assent in the West, and that instigated revolutionary developments. The culture of the time was responding to abuses in power between the monarchy, the privileges of the nobility, and the political power embedded in the hierarchy of the Catholic Church.

There were prior developments regarding reason throughout the history of culture and our human ability to think. Humanism altered the focus in our lives of including God and then only relying on our own interpretation and reason. The system of thought known as Scholasticism, culminating in the work of St. Thomas Aquinas, resurrected reason as a tool of understanding faith but subordinated it to spiritual revelation.

Pope Saint John Paul II, in his 1998 encyclical, *"Fides et Ratio, Faith and Reason"* said St. Thomas "had the great merit of giving pride of place to the harmony which exists between faith and reason," knowing that "both the light of reason and the light of faith come from God... Hence there can be no contradiction between them." (FR, 43) The Enlightenment gave birth to the concept that our reality was a construct of our biological existence. Under this way of thinking, there is no Truth beyond our subjective experience; all reality or Truth is simply contained in our senses. I am reminded of the old

The Truth of Love Through the Truth of Suffering

riddle, "if a tree falls in the forest and no one is around, does it make a sound?" Once we "die" our senses are extinguished through death. When we are extinguished, then our being is extinguished. Therefore, no senses – no being – no God – no eternity – no Truth! But Truth agrees with reality. Our emotions and opinions are not reality, they are emotions and opinions. We can share these randomly and explicitly in the media, and we do, and we have become rude, offensive, etc.! Feelings, opinions, are not fact.

The Catechism of the Catholic Church states:

> The dignity of the human person is rooted in his creation in the image and likeness of God; it is fulfilled in his vocation to divine beatitude. It is essential to a human being freely to direct himself to this fulfillment. By his deliberate actions, the human person does, or does not, conform to the good promised by God and attested by moral conscience. Human beings make their own contribution to their interior growth; they make their whole sentient and spiritual lives into means of this growth. With the help of grace, they

grow in virtue, avoid sin, and if they sin they entrust themselves as did the prodigal son[1] to the mercy of our Father in heaven. In this way they attain to the perfection of charity. (CCC, 1700)

The definition of free will is the power of the will to determine itself and to act of itself, without any compulsion from within or coercion from without. It is the faculty of an intelligent being to act or not act, to act this way or another way. St. Augustine, the Angelic Doctor of the Church, says our free choice of the will assumes that there can be no denying that we have a will. He explains it as "a will by which we seek to live a good and upright life and to attain unto perfect wisdom" (pg. 128).

Jean Valjean, in *Les Misérables*, is so transformed by the Bishop's merciful gesture that it changes the direction of his life from that point on and his IDENTITY becomes that of MERCY in action in order to absorb the impact of the mercy that has been extended to him when he felt so undeserving. It exposed the natural law that was dead within him because of what had befallen him, from the trials and events compounded on his soul in the suffering, injustice, and evil that prevailed in his entire life up until that day. The Natural Law resides ontologically in us. It is part of our nature – it was we are made for, a truth that resonates in our soul. It is our very being.

In our imaging of Christ, we learn to become more like Christ. We follow his example to us of how He acted as He was in our human form. Even in suffering as suffering becomes a participation in the mystery of Christ. Suffering is his way of "becoming like him (Christ) in his death" so that he "may attain the resurrection from the dead." (Philippians 3:10 & 11) Through suffering, we participate in the crucifixion of Christ. Because we are being saved and redeemed, through the suffering, death, and resurrection of Christ we can "participate" in his Passion with the guarantee of the Resurrection.

The first thing the next morning I called my sister Cheri to come with me to take Regina to the children's hospital. I did not tell Regina what I was planning. I was unsure about everything. I didn't know what to do to save her. One hospital had already turned her away and two doctors had missed the obvious signs of her being in a deadly crisis. As my sister was coming down the road I was in the driveway with Regina because she wanted to go to school. I got her in the car and my sister instinctively followed behind me. As I drove in a direction away from the school, Regina became frantic and then hysterical once she realized where I was taking her. She smashed my phone and attempted to jump out of the moving car. I wondered what my sister was experiencing driving behind us, watching Regina's behavior ahead of her.

We pulled into the ER at the children's hospital and she was exploding with rage and anguish. I don't know how we got her in the door, but as I sat her down with my sister she calmed down. I told them at the desk that my daughter was in crisis and needed to see a doctor as fast as possible or she could bolt from the hospital and could potentially hurt herself. They got us promptly into a treatment room. As they took her vitals, I called her father and her brother, who immediately came. A female doctor eventually came in and examined Regina, and when she was finished, she walked out the door and I followed directly behind her. I followed her into her cubicle and she turned, startled. I simply asked, "Did you look under her gown?" She replied, "Oh yes, this little girl is going nowhere!" Relief hit me, though all my feelings were solidly frozen inside my body. I knew a doctor had finally seen the truth!

Regina was in the ER for three days, as there were no beds for her. They gave her an around-the-clock mental health aide to sit by her bed, due to her saying she wanted to die or hurt herself. They assembled a team of three beautiful women: her pediatrician, a psychiatrist, and a social worker. They consulted with

The Truth of Love Through the Truth of Suffering

us daily and attempted to stabilize her low heart rate. They gave her ongoing snacks and drinks that she refused to eat. And they searched diligently for the next step in saving her life.

On the third day, her father and I were called to the Psychiatrist's office. As we walked through the corridors, I prayed for an answer to some kind of treatment for her. The psychiatrist did not have good news. She told us there was no way to transport our daughter out of the county, and there were few treatment places available, and they did not know any options right now for her. It was all completely confusing, and related to insurance, and terrifying. We left the office. I was in despair; every hope we had was destroyed in this meeting. As one of the large automatic doors opened inward, instead of outward, I walked directly into it and it slammed into my eyebrow, leaving a bleeding gash. We still hurried back to our daughter, my physical pain mocking the emotional pain in my soul. As we came around the last corner, her "team" was standing outside of her doorway. As we walked up, they looked at my bleeding head. Her pediatrician said, "We got her a placement at Miami Children's Hospital. They have a juvenile ED floor and a bed for her." We found out later that the person in charge of that floor had interned under the pediatrician, and that is how

Regina got a bed! I walked through the hospital to the ER to have my head stitched up flooded with too many emotions to even feel the pain. I could feel God working now, perhaps, finding a direction for this journey for Regina.

The Truth of Love Through the Truth of Suffering

Dr. Sue Ellen Nolan

> "And after you have suffered a little while, the God of all grace, who has called you to his eternal glory in Christ, will himself restore, support, strengthen, and establish you."
> 1 Peter 5:10

> "Those who share in Christ's sufferings have before their eyes the Paschal Mystery of the Cross and Resurrection, in which Christ descends, in a first phase, to the ultimate limits of human weakness and impotence: indeed, he dies nailed to the Cross. But if at the same time in this weakness there is accomplished his *lifting up*, confirmed by the power of the Resurrection, then this means that the weaknesses of all human sufferings are capable of being infused with the same power of God manifested in Christ's Cross."
> Salvifici Doloris, 23

The Principles:

During this time of suffering, fear, grief, and great trial in dealing with my daughter's disease, God revealed clear principles of suffering well. In Pope Saint John Paul II's apostolic letter, *Salvifici Doloris*, there are themes or principles that illuminate to us the mystery of suffering. God also revealed, in the example of His obedient Son, in His life and in His walk to the cross, practical steps on *how to suffer well*. These three practical steps have set into motion a paradigm shift on how we are meant to confront our own *Gospel of Suffering* each time we are forced to reconsider it.

These principles and practical steps will change everything you know about suffering, and reveal to you God's ultimate plan in accompanying you *on that long road* that winds through suffering.

Dr. Sue Ellen Nolan

"In this you rejoice, even if now for a little while you have had to suffer various trials, so that the genuineness of your faith—being more precious than gold that, though tested by fire—may be found to result in praise and glory and hope when Jesus Christ is revealed."

1 Peter 1: 6 & 7

"The cross will not crush you. If its weight makes you stagger, its power will also sustain you."

St Padre Pio

Principle One: God Took the Greatest Evil and Made it the Greatest Good

Christ, fully Divine and fully human, was crucified on the Cross for the redemption of all of mankind. His death would have been just an execution if it hadn't contained the power of the redemption and the Resurrection. The greatest evil ever done was the crucifixion of Christ, yet God had a perfect plan in it that culminated in the Resurrection. The cross became part of the solution to suffering and evil by our Creator's perfect plan.

Peter Kreeft says in *"Fundamentals of the Faith"* that the problem of evil in the world is the main reason for people turning from God and abandoning faith. He writes:

> He has lifted the curtain on the problem of evil with Christ. There, the greatest evil that ever

happened, both the greatest spiritual evil and the greatest physical evil, both the greatest sin (deicide) and the greatest suffering (perfect love hated and crucified), is revealed as His wise and loving plan to bring about the greatest good, the salvation of the world from sin and suffering eternally"(1998, pgs. 54-58).

The Cross is part of the solution to definitive evil in our world, which is the definitive loss of salvation, and eternal separation from God. The resurrection is the embodiment of success in transforming, thereafter, all evil into good, when we bring God into it.

Christ's mission strikes at evil, which is bound to sin and death. We "perish" when we lose eternal life. Jesus was given to humanity, and conquered sin and death to restore us to our relationship to God so that we may have eternal life and avoid definitive suffering, the loss of salvation. By His salvific work Christ *"blots out* from human history *the dominion of sin...* and gives man the possibility of living in Sanctifying Grace." In this victory over sin, *"He also takes away the dominion of death, by His resurrection."* (SD, 14 & 15)

The Truth of Love Through the Truth of Suffering

Christ's mission was the will of His Father in restoring us to our relationship to God, so that we may have eternal life and avoid definitive suffering. He came to do the will of His Father for each and every one of us. His endeavor grants us hope and throws a new light upon every suffering and can radically change our perspective on suffering. And even influence our experience.

As my mom was succumbing to dementia, I could not comprehend being on the other side of not having my mother here anymore and I spent a couple of years praying desperately for her. I found a priest, Fr. Dennis Cooney, to give me counsel, and as it turns out his own mother had passed away from Alzheimer's just a couple of years back. Our God is providential! I met with Fr. Cooney, whenever I needed support in dealing with this merciless disease, for about two years while he guided me through this disease and he encouraged me to always pray for a holy death for my mother. My prayers were heard by God and answered in beautiful ways.

One Saturday, which turned out to be the very last day that my mother was conscious on this Earth, I sat on my mom's bed alongside my niece Lori Ann. Lori and I were very close in age and had been raised together. I told people we were close like twins, since I already had a bunch of sisters. We sat on the bed and told my mother stories of the fun things we had done with her and my second oldest sister, Gail, Lori's mother, driving the back roads on a summer afternoon, going out camping with a group of girls, driving around to look at the Christmas lights, and many other memories. She lay there in her hospital bed and smiled along with every story, no longer able to use words. Her sweet, beautiful blue eyes reflected the happiness we held in the memories of our childhood. Later that afternoon my mother's eyes would close, never to open again as she slipped into unconsciousness.

Most of us had all been there those last days, observing our mother as she seemed to move between the physical world and the spiritual one. It felt as if we were watching miracles. We had heard her talk of angels in the room. We had heard her speak of seeing her beloved father coming to get her in a boat, to take her "across the river." She was animated and enraptured. We heard her talk of "the baby," which we assumed meant our brother Darrell, whom she had lost at birth after our father returned from World War II. The room seemed filled with the light of hope and of eternal love, and we floated in and out of the room, pausing to talk in wonder about what she was saying. My siblings, cousins, nieces, and nephews wept in awe of the obvious experience of being with her in this world as we witnessed her fading into the next.

That night, after my mother had slipped into a coma, I was in the room with two of my sisters. My sister Brenda was reading a book and my sister Debbie was dozing on the sofa. Our mom had a rosary around her neck made from little stones from the mountain at Medjugorje. Brenda had put it there though she wasn't Catholic. My mom wasn't Catholic either but her favorite person growing up had been her grandfather and he often took her to Mass with him when she was very little. She'd been wearing it all the time we were keeping vigil in her room. I told my sister that I wanted to pray the Rosary and she nodded in agreement. It was late at night in a nursing home, so it was very peaceful and quiet. I snuggled into my mom's side on the bed with her and I began to pray, taking each little stone into my fingers as I completed each decade.

My mom had been unconscious now for six or seven hours, completely unresponsive in her coma. But as I began to pray the rosary, she began to move and make sounds. I continued to pray, watching her, and she continued to make gentle noises and made attempts to move, though her body was unable to cooperate. It's hard to put into words what we witnessed; but if you can, imagine someone in a state of unconsciousness responding to your voice. Brenda put her book down and sat up slowly, while Debbie was suddenly alert, her dozing forgotten. They barely breathed as I prayed very slowly and purposefully through each decade of the Rosary. My mom responded the entire time. When I concluded the rosary, she stopped moving and responding, and she was gone to us again. We sat in wonderment. There was power in that prayer for her.

My mom was progressing towards death but God was showing up and showing His plan as it unwound in front of us. We were witnesses to God working in the evil that my mother was succumbing to, an evil that would take her out of our lives. He was making this greatest evil for us, her children, a greater good as He took her home to a place where she was healthy and whole, and surrounded by loved ones who had gone before her. We could only attempt to imagine what it was like, as she gave us a glimpse of the journey.

Father Emmanuelle Cueto Ramos is a 31-year-old priest who lives in Peru. In February 2020 he developed a brain tumor that was initially benign. Unfortunately, restrictions due to the Covid-19 pandemic kept him from getting treatment until August, and by that time the tumor had progressed to stage-three malignant cancer and was inoperable.

Father Emmanuelle was given only months to live. He was rendered blind by the tumor but he lived out his priestly vocation, and his remaining time on Earth, in joy and hope.

Fr. Ramos accepted this suffering "for the Church, for what is happening in the Church today." He announced:

> "Whatever time God gives me; I'll live it to the maximum with a smile on my face. I define it as my splendid Calvary, which the Lord is allowing me to offer to Him. I want to go directly to heaven and suffering is the quickest way to become a Saint" (Picón, *Aleteia*, 2020).

In his last tweets published in July, Father Emmanuelle Cueto wrote: "For someone who wants to be a saint, suffer. It is not optional, but an essential assumption, that it is an opportunity to sanctify and save oneself. And death, seen with the Christian eye, is expected; but when death is seen with the human gaze, it is feared."

Fr. Ramos died on Saturday, March 27, 2021 having suffered courageously for souls and the Church.

According to Pope Saint John Paul II, there is a special call to courage and fortitude which is sustained by the eloquence of the event of the Resurrection (SD, 25). Our beloved Pope says:

> Those who share in Christ's suffering have before their eyes the Paschal Mystery of the Cross and Resurrection, in which Christ descends, in the first place, to the ultimate limits of human weakness and impotence... in this weakness there is accomplished His lifting up, confirmed by the power of the Resurrection, then this means that all the weaknesses of all human sufferings are capable of being infused with the same power of God manifested in Christ's cross.

He continues:

...the theme of this "birth of power in weakness" this spiritual tempering of man in the midst of trials and tribulations... is the particular vocation of those who share in Christ's sufferings. (SD, 23)

The Truth of Love Through the Truth of Suffering

"For just as the sufferings of Christ are abundant for us, so also our consolation is abundant through Christ. If we are being afflicted it is for your consolation and salvation; if we are being consoled, it is for your consolation, which you experience when you patiently endure the same sufferings that we are suffering."

2 Corinthians 3-7

"If you wish to come where I am going, that is, to glory, you must come this road, that is, through thorns."

St Philip Neri

Principle Two: Suffering was Used as the Tool for our Salvation

We know that through the cross sin and death were redeemed. The tool of our redemption was Christ's suffering. Only Christ is capable of embracing the measure of evil contained in the sin of man, in every sin, and in total sin, (from the beginning of time and to the end of time). Suffering was redeemed on the cross as well.

According to Pope St John Paul II's anthropology we are created in the image of God, with a soul that is bound up in the good of God. We have the ability to obtain the likeness of Christ by following Him in what He revealed to us in His walk on this earth. We are created with a body and a mind as well. Within our mind, our intellect we have free-will, a gift that offers us the ability to choose God in obedience according to what is revealed in Scripture. Our body, as a temple of the Holy Spirit, is meant to seek God. These elements form us in indelible dignity, just for existing as a human being made for eternal life, from the moment of conception. We have value in BEING – created in a calling out of love, in the Image and Likeness of God – and we have VALUE in existing, period.

Our existence calls us to seek the Truth, and the Truth is God. When we encounter God we are led to obedience and sacrifice in our faith. This includes suffering redemptively. We LOVE in being OBEDIENT, as Jesus was, fully human and fully divine, and in uniting our suffering to His cross it is elevated in the transforming power of the miracle of His sacrifice. Through suffering Christ became our hero so we can use our suffering to also become heroic. As Venerable Bishop Sheen stated, "Pain without Christ is suffering; Pain with Christ is Sacrifice."

Pope Saint John Paul II wrote in *Redemptor Hominis, The Redeemer of Man,* (RH) his first Encyclical after becoming Pope, on Jesus:

> Jesus Christ, the Son of the living God, became our reconciliation with the Father. It was He, and he alone, who satisfied the Father's eternal love, that fatherhood that from the beginning found expression in creating the world, giving man all the riches of creation, and making

him "little less than God," in that he was created "in the image and after the likeness of God." He and He alone also satisfied that fatherhood of God and that love which man in a way rejected by breaking the first Covenant and the later covenants that God "again and again offered to man." The redemption of the world — this tremendous mystery of love in which creation is renewed — is, at its deepest root, the fullness of justice in a human Heart — the Heart of the First-born Son — in order that it may become justice in the hearts of many human beings, predestined from eternity in the Firstborn Son to be children of God and called to grace, called to love. The Cross on Calvary, through which Jesus Christ — a Man, the Son of the Virgin Mary, thought to be the son of Joseph of Nazareth — "leaves" this world, is also a fresh manifestation of the eternal fatherhood of God, who in him draws near again to humanity, to each human being, giving him the thrice-holy "Spirit of truth." (RH, 48-55)

There's a very recent story about a young priest named Father John Hallowell, who, when the abuse scandal broke again, had such deep, heartfelt trauma related to what was happening within the church, said, "I prayed in 2018 that if there was some suffering I could undertake on behalf of all the victims, some cross I could carry, I would welcome that."

Father Hallowell, barely a year later at the age of 40 unexpectedly suffered what they thought was a stroke. He went to the Mayo Clinic for a brain scan, which revealed a tumor. He has a good prognosis, and says he will embrace his cross willingly. He asked for victims of the abuse scandal to send their names to him, and he will offer up his chemo and surgery in their names. Father Hollowell says he is very much at peace now, though he endured brain surgery in March of 2020 and is in ongoing treatment with chemotherapy. (*Aleteia, 2020*) This is redemptive suffering.

St. Paul writes in Galatians, "May I never boast of anything except the cross of our Lord Jesus Christ, by which the world has been crucified to me, and I to the world." (Galatians 6:14) Suffering is a vocation (SD, 26) *with a special call to courage and fortitude,* (SD,

25) and with a *particular power that draws a person interiorly close to Christ*. Christ, by suffering salvifically is present is every human suffering, and can act from within that suffering by the powers of His spirit of Truth, His consoling Spirit. (SD, 26)

Dr. Sue Ellen Nolan

"For this slight momentary affliction is preparing us for an eternal weight of glory beyond all measure because we look not at what can be seen but at what cannot be seen"

2 Corinthians 4:17 & 18

"You ask me whether I am in good spirits. How could I not be so? As long as Faith gives me strength I will always be joyful!"

Blessed Pier Giorgio Frassati

Principle Three: There Can Be Joy in Your Gospel of Suffering

When suffering is perceived as useless there is depression and despair. When suffering is united to Christ's redemption on the Cross joy can be found in overcoming the sense of the uselessness in suffering. St Paul expresses joy as he writes: "I am now rejoicing in my sufferings for your sake" while he is "completing what is lacking Christ's afflictions for the sake of his body, that is, the Church." (Colossians 1: 24) Our Pope John Paul II declares that this joy, so personally shared by Paul of Tarsus, is valid for everyone who finds themselves "at the end of the long road that winds through suffering which forms part of the history of man and which is illuminated by the Word of God." (SD, 1) This expression of joy comes in the discovery that there is a saving value in suffering! "But wait a minute," you might ask, "did you say joy in suffering?" Yes!

Christ transforms this feeling and brings an interior certainty of the salvific power of the suffering person when they are "completing what is lacking in Christ's afflictions." (Colossians 1: 24) What lacks in Christ's perfect suffering? Nothing from Him. He completes fully, intentionally, divinely, humanly, and perfectly. But in his anthropology of being both fully Human and fully Divine, He elevates his suffering to the divine and the supernatural:

> Christ, the son, who is consubstantial with the Father, suffers as a man. His suffering has human dimensions; it also has — unique in the history of humanity — a depth and intensity which, while being human, can also be an incomparable depth and intensity of suffering in so far as the man who suffers is in person the only begotten son Himself God from God. Therefore, only he — the only begotten son — is capable of embracing the measure of evil contained in the sin of man in every sin and in total sin, according to the dimension of the historical existence of humanity on earth. (SD, 17)

Two natures were required. Our Savior had to be fully human and fully divine. He therefore brings the Divine down to our nature and also elevates our nature to the Divine.

I can remember one instance of finding joy in suffering, during my Regina's battle with anorexia. The day finally came when Regina would be transported across the state to Miami Children's Hospital. We waited patiently and she acquiesced to being in the hospital. Her control over restricting food had not been challenged as they had not "tube fed" her. Toward the end of the day, they said the ambulance was ready and she was taken down to it on a stretcher.

She was in surprisingly good spirits as we headed across Alligator Alley. There was a driver and a paramedic on board. At one point the paramedic queried, "Mom, does her heart rate usually run low?" I knew nothing about her normal heart rate. I shrugged at him. "It's running low, like the 30s and 40s." That was my first glimpse into what an eating disorder does to a physical body internally.

When we reached Miami Children's Hospital, Regina was placed on the 4th floor, the Eating Disorders unit. It was mid-November, and as we faced the ongoing hospital stay to stabilize Regina's critically low heart rate due to her anorexia, the Thanksgiving holiday was upon us. It was a hard contradiction that my daughter was struggling with a battle of controlling food when this was the holiday focused around a major meal. Her mealtime had become a sacred, private act of dismantling the demons that kept her in control of denying all nourishment to feed her body. I was not invited to the event. And it sometimes was hours long. At her breakfast time on Thanksgiving morning, I attended Mass in the small chapel. I needed God as close to me as I could have Him to sustain me. I spontaneously asked the hospital chaplain if we could have a special blessing on that day. Later, we were sitting in the floor's family room when I saw the chaplain walk in. I was so happy to see him; he heard my confession and then went to my daughter and heard hers. He then did a short prayer service and gave us both a special blessing. My heart was overflowing with God; I was filled with an unearthly joy that was a contradiction to our struggle against death. And He became all I needed to get through that day and to hang on to the hope in my daughter's survival.

But God didn't stop there. He is a God after our hearts; He desires to prove He is real and that He is affecting our lives. Later on, I sat by myself in the family room feeling very lonely on our first

The Truth of Love Through the Truth of Suffering

Thanksgiving ever away from family, with the irony that I wouldn't even get to share my meal with my daughter. I sat there fighting the sadness and grief when I heard some commotion outside the door. I looked out to see a group in matching jackets with many young people channeling down the hallway carrying shopping bags. As they got closer, I read the name off the jacket of the first young man: Church of the Little Flower. They were from the Youth Group there. A couple of boys gathered around me as I waved to them and a couple of adults came over. The boy handed me a bag containing a full Thanksgiving dinner for one! I felt the providential love of God, my Father! I told the boys through tears that they had answered my prayers, as I had no Thanksgiving meal to eat that day, and their beautiful faces had made God real for me! I asked the boys to please pray for my young daughter who was there in the next room battling for her life. The leader took my hands and the boys gathered around and they prayed out loud for my baby girl, by name. God became real for me in the form of these youth working for Him. I needed nothing else. Like Job, I did not concern myself any longer with the suffering of the moment. I could endure. I could persevere. My Lord had shown Himself! He had my girl. He had me. He is real. I can do this. This suffering was infused with joy!

It is in this light that we should see the sufferings of this life, and why they are not only to be borne with patience but, if one can by grace muster it, even accepted with joy. As Saint Peter, the first Pope, told us, "But rejoice insofar as you share Christ's sufferings, that you may also rejoice and be glad when His glory is revealed." (1 Peter 4:13)

Now, joy is a strong word. Joy is a challenging word when we think of suffering. When we truly can surrender and unite ourselves to it, there is something that happens in suffering. In a counter-intuitive way, amid tremendous suffering, we can find ourselves laughing, sometimes even at ourselves. Oftentimes others can bring inexplicable humor and laughter into the moment in stark and direct contrast to what we are enduring.

Cale Clarke, a Catholic apologist on Relevant Radio, in "The Importance of Both Grief and Joy" defines the difference between happiness and joy as when the "balloon of promise gets popped by the pin of life." He says happiness depends on what's happening, it depends on what is going on in your life. But joy is more than that; it doesn't depend on the circumstances, and it's not the absence of struggles in your life – and it comes from a relationship with God.

The Truth of Love Through the Truth of Suffering

Father Cooney talked in a Spiritual Direction with me about happiness being attainable on this earth. We are made for happiness, and we find the full revelation of happiness in God, but joy is divine! Joy is a transcendent emotion from the life of Christ living within our souls, no matter what's happening in our lives.

Dr. Sue Ellen Nolan

"And the Lord answered Job out of the storm and said: Gird up your loins now like a man. I will question you and you will tell me the answers!"
Job 40:6&7

"The poverty in the West is a different kind of poverty — it is not only a poverty of loneliness but also of spirituality. There's a hunger for love, as there is a hunger for God."
Saint Mother Teresa of Calcutta

Principle Four: God is God and We are Not; But When God Shows Up, We Can Do This!

Job, in his immeasurable suffering, demanded an answer from our Lord. And it was given in the revelation of His Godliness and glory. In their relationship God was asking the question of Job that Jesus would ask His Disciples, "Who do you say that I am?" (Matthew 16:15)

This is the formula for our relationship with God. He answers us with Himself! And when we know He is real; we can go on. God reveals Himself when we draw near to Him in our need for him. He answers us in our hearts. He tells us He is God, and we are not. Think: relationship with God! Henri de Lubac wrote:

> "And the strangest and deepest of hurts become possible, within this unique form of association…; when there even exists a power so strong

and so deep reaching that merely to submit to it, even with patience is simply not enough-that we have to consent personally and willingly to what would be a violation at the hands of any other power." (Love Alone is Credible, 2004, pg. 146)

We can submit to God when we have a relationship with Him. When this 'great Being', God, comes into our lives and shows Himself, and we draw near to Him, we can endure suffering! He has proven that He has us. God is asking us the same question posed to Job, "Who do you say that I am"? In our spiritual poverty we can answer that question.

Spiritual poverty allows us to abandon ourselves to the Divine Providence of God our Father. All of us are "poor" in that we are dependent beings. We didn't bring ourselves into existence and at some time we will die. We don't hold the universe together. We cannot grant ourselves eternal life. When we sin, we can't give ourselves forgiveness. In all these things, we are dependent on God.

So, poverty of spirit means knowing your need for God. It means being open to what God can do for you. It means knowing that He will come for you. That He will show up, because we need Him, and nothing else will suffice.

Suffering allows us to see ourselves as we are, by revealing to us in our "weakness and emptying of self," that at the end of the day, and at the end of our lives, we are totally and utterly dependent upon God. (SD, 23)

We also know about Adam's Original Solitude in his knowledge of his anthropology, that God was God, and that he was not. He knew that he was not one of the animals that God had created and had called him into dominion over. Adam felt this solitude, which is separateness, or loneliness. God loved Adam so much, as He loves us, that He answered his prayer even before he could form it in his head! In his heart, Adam felt the loss of "likeness" that he could not even conceptualize, and God answered his prayer before it went from his heart to his head. He put him to sleep and removed from him a rib. He then called into being a "helpmate" and companion for Adam: woman. He gave Adam the desire of his heart before his head could fully understand his need.

God is the God of the book of Job who answered Job with his God-ness. He answers us as well and he meets us in our solitude and suffering, at the center of our need. Sometimes before we can even ask. Just like

He did with Adam. And sometimes we have to demand, like Job did.

Humankind's story is the story of Adam and Eve. There is both good and evil in their story. By eating from the Tree of the Knowledge of Good and Evil they usurped God's place. In their error and sin they used their free will to be like God themselves. The *Catechism of the Catholic Church* states:

> Of all visible creatures only man is "able to know and love his creator." He is "the only creature on earth that God has willed for its own sake," and he alone is called to share, by knowledge and love, in God's own life. It was for this end that he was created, and this is the fundamental reason for his dignity: what made you establish man in so great a dignity? Certainly, the incalculable love by which you have looked on your creature in yourself! You are taken with love for her; for by love indeed you created her, by love you have given her a being capable of tasting your eternal Good. (CCC, 356)

Being in the image of God the human individual possesses the dignity of a person, who is not just something, but someone. We are capable of self-knowledge, of self-possession, and of freely giving ourselves and entering into communion with other persons. And we are called by grace to a covenant with our Creator, to offer Him a response of faith and love that no other creature can give in our stead.

God created everything for humankind, but we, in turn, were created to serve and love God and to offer all creation back to Him, as stated in the Catechism of the Catholic Church:

> What is it that is about to be created, that enjoys such honor? It is man that great and wonderful living creature, more precious in the eyes of God than all other creatures! For him, the heavens and the earth, the sea, and all the rest of creation exist. God attached so much importance to his salvation that he did not spare his own Son for the sake of man. Nor does he ever cease to work, trying every possible means, until he has raised man up to himself and made him sit at his right hand. (CCC, 358)

Dr. Sue Ellen Nolan

The treatment Regina received at Miami Children's Hospital had medically stabilized her. The next step was long-term treatment for her eating disorder. EDs, especially anorexia, have an incredibly high mortality rate. We were slowly being educated in the terrifying reality of this illness. Placements for treatment depended on insurance and availability. On the Sunday after Thanksgiving, our determined social worker at MCH found us a placement in an adolescent treatment center in Arizona. We were to be discharged on Monday. My sister Cheri and niece Becky picked us up and drove us home to pack a bag. We left the following morning for Tampa International Airport to fly to a mountain town in Arizona. We arrived in the late afternoon in Phoenix and Bill, the van driver for Rosewood, an Adolescent Treatment Center in Wickenburg, held a sign up with our last name on it, as we picked up our checked baggage. We climbed into the van and began the journey through Phoenix and up into the mountains to Rosewood, in the mountains, by the Hassayampa River.

Regina was pensive but relaxed. The road changed from flat desert to cactus and wildlife-filled hills and then mountains. It grew very dark and much colder. We arrived at the facility around 10:00 pm. Walking inside I noticed a courtyard area with buildings on three sides, forming a roughly "U" shape. We were told that it used to be a dude ranch and it was a western as your imagination could picture. After the tour, we were taken to the community room where the children were decorating a Christmas tree. They greeted us as we came in, twelve of them, in varying degrees of different eating disorders. My daughter became immediately comfortable with them, possibly recognizing their torment as her own.

We had completed the paperwork with our social worker prior to arriving, so I was told to say goodbye to my daughter. I hugged her and left her. The director held my arm in hers as I was ushered out of the facility. But I was to leave, and leave my daughter to herself. Regina was 13 years old, and had never been away from me for more than four or five days. She was fighting literally for her life, and I had to leave her alone and fly 2,300 miles home, not having any way of knowing if she would live or die.

Once I was back in the van, Bill, who had been chatty with us on the trip up, left me to myself. As we crossed the Hassayampa River he asked me if I would like to tour the town of Wickenburg. He said the children earned passes to go into town for special events and it was a rugged, Old West town. Despite feeling numb from leaving Regina behind and jet-lagged — my body thought it was three hours ahead— I agreed. Bill drove me through all the historical places in the area, speaking animatedly in the dark. We passed a Catholic church and he asked me if I was Catholic. I nodded. He asked me randomly if I believed in apparitions of Our Lady, like Our Lady of Medjugorje. I looked at him and said yes.

Bill began to tell me a story. He said he had been a member of the Knights of Columbus and they had held a raffle. The prize was a trip to Medjugorje. The man who won it could not go, so Bill bought the trip from him. Bill told me that in the village of Medjugorje he had experienced healing from an addiction, which completely changed his life. When he came home, his conversion was so awesome and phenomenal that his parents asked him to take his sister, who was struggling with her own deep personal problems, on a pilgrimage to Medjugorje, and while there she received healing as well. Bill's parents then made the decision themselves to go to Medjugorje. The entire family went. During their time there, he explained, his parents got into an argument in the village. Bill's father became verbally abusive, and for the first time in his life, Bill put his father in his place and told him he was out of line and had to stop. Afterward, during the Mass, his father felt a blackness leaving him and he came home healed of a darkness that had plagued him for years. Within a period of time, he developed cancer and Bill quit his job to care for him. Each day they would pray the rosary together until the day that his father died.

Driving down the small mountain road in the middle of the night, in the bleak darkness, after I had left my young daughter at a treatment center I could feel that God was doing something. I began to tell Bill the story of how Our Lady of Medjugorje told me Regina would be born. I told him all the details as I held back the tears. After I was finished Bill reached down and pulled from his pocket a black rosary. He put it in my hand, and told me Regina's story was renewing his faith at that moment and he wanted me to have it. It was the rosary he had prayed with his father as he was living his last months of life. Soon we pulled up to the hotel where I would spend a couple of hours before my flight back to Florida. I was elated with the love of God. I was in the heart of His mother, and I was being given a profound sign that God was in this, still.

Pope Saint John Paul II wrote:

> As a result of Christ's salvific work, man exists on earth *with the hope* of eternal life and holiness. And even though the victory over sin and death achieved by Christ in his Cross and Resurrection does not abolish

temporal suffering from human life, nor free from suffering the whole historical dimension of human existence, it nevertheless *throws a new light* upon this dimension and upon every suffering: the light of salvation. This is the light of the Gospel, that is, of the Good News. At the heart of this light is the truth expounded in the conversation with Nicodemus: "For God so loved the world that he gave his only Son." This truth radically changes the picture of man's history and his earthly situation: despite the sin that took root in this history both as an original inheritance and as the "sin of the world" and as the sum of personal sins, God the Father has loved the only-begotten Son, that is, he loves him in a lasting way; and then in time, precisely through this all-surpassing love, he "gives" this Son, that he may strike at the very roots of human evil and thus draw close in a salvific way to the whole world of suffering in which man shares." (SD, 15)

I had a radical change in the way that I suffered, in the midst of one of the most traumatic times of my life. There was a new light that shone, literally in that darkness, and Christ loved me in His "all-surpassing love," this time through His mother. He came down, to live and die, to share an intimate relationship with me, and He was my solace in suffering because He loved me this much!

One of my friends, Patty, lost her husband a year or so ago. I went to the funeral and she invited me to come visit her in the next little while. Suffering is intimidating and I showed up at her house expecting to console her. We sat down and we started talking. She told me of the different stories of what God had done during that time and, though she was grieving terribly, He had walked her through it in very powerful ways. Her cousin had come down the week of her first Valentine's Day alone. She had put her house on the market for sale, and he was going to help her with getting the house ready for the realtor. They discussed what to do with the yard and especially some hibiscus bushes that appeared to be dead. He was going to dig them up for her and plant something else.

The next morning as they were having coffee on the lanai, she was sitting with her back to the hibiscus bush. He looked in that direction and began to smile. She turned around and couldn't believe her eyes: there, on the supposedly dead hibiscus bush, were two massive yellow flowers. Later, when she and I saw each other next, she showed me pictures of them she had taken on her phone, and told me that her husband, through the entire 35 years of their marriage, always gave her yellow flowers. She knew God was shoring her up tremendously in this time of loss. During her Gospel of Suffering, in revealing His presence in her life He brought her the consolation of a gift from her husband for Valentine's Day.

Love is manifested in suffering when we have a relationship with God and we surrender, even our suffering, to His will; when we assent to His will, because we want only HIS will in our lives, God will show us He is real, and in charge.

God gave us His only son to set us free from evil or suffering, not end it in our lives. This sacrifice "bears within itself the definitive and absolute perspective on suffering. And in this, love is manifested, the infinite love both of that only-begotten Son and of the Father, who for this reason 'gives' His Son. This is love for man, love for the world: it is salvific love."(SD, 14)

The Truth of Love Through the Truth of Suffering

Dr. Sue Ellen Nolan

"For God so loved the world, that he gave his only Son, that whoever believes in him should not perish but have eternal life."

John 3:16

"Suffering in itself does not make us holy, it is only when we unite it, out of love, the suffering Christ that it has meaning. Suffering without love is wasted pain."

Mother Angelica

"Man cannot fully find himself except through a sincere gift of himself."

Gaudium et Spes, 24

Principle Five: Suffering Unleashes Love and Evokes Action

Suffering has been opened up to love because Christ has opened His suffering to man. (SD, 20) St. Paul admonishes us to "direct your hearts to the love of God and to the steadfastness of Christ (2 Thessalonians 3:5) and to "present your bodies as a living sacrifice" (Romans 12:1). Christ is united to us through the Cross. We can respond to this love, with love, as Christ lives in the one with whom He loves in this way. This path of Paul's is purely Paschal, enlightened by sharing in the Cross with Christ, through the experience of the Risen One. (SD, 21)

Pope Saint John Paul II says:

> "Christ's resurrection has revealed 'the glory of the future age' and, at the same time, He has confirmed 'the boast of the Cross: "the *glory that is hidden in the very suffering of*

> *Christ* and which has been and is often mirrored in human suffering, as an expression of man's spiritual greatness." (SD, 22)

Saint Paul then boasts gladly of his weakness, so that the power of Christ may rest upon him. (2 Corinthians 12:9) He courageously claims in Timothy, "And therefore I suffer as I do. But I am not ashamed, for I know whom I have believed" (2 Timothy 1:12). In this "Gospel *paradox of weakness and strength*," (SD, 22) we have before us the Cross and the Resurrection, where our weakness is lifted up, "then this means that the weaknesses of all human sufferings are capable of being infused with the same power of God manifested in Christ's cross," a "birth of power in weakness." (SD, 23) This "meaning makes itself known together with *'the working of God's love.'*" (SD, 23)

In our weakness we can love our Creator Who redeemed us with His Son. We are lifted up into this love, elevated into the Paschal Mystery of eternal love and untainted to this love, which manifests in strength! In this love we ultimately make our way back to ourselves, in suffering; back to our soul. "The more he shares in this love, man rediscovers himself more and more fully in suffering: he rediscovers the 'soul' which he had thought he had "lost" because of suffering." (SD, 23)

Just a couple of years ago two of my friends, Marcus and Connie, lost their only son, Andy, on New Year's Eve, in a horrible accident on an isolated road in the middle of Michigan. Andy was hanging out with a group of people, who were acquaintances, partying for New Years. The sketchy details of the accident came out after the fact and after Connie and Marcus began an investigation into what actually happened to Andy the night of the accident. There was a Snapchat photo of Andy smiling in the passenger seat, sent that night, while the someone else was driving his truck. A renowned crime scene reconstructionist found there was another vehicle involved. One of the guys who was there had a truck that had, suspiciously, been sent to be demolished. In the investigation, the truck was discovered and paint marks were found on the truck and tires, that were the same color as Andy's truck. It appeared that his truck had run Andy's truck off the road possibly causing the accident.

Connie and Marcus were left with no recourse, since a criminal investigation was not initiated, so they pursued a civil case naming those who were with Andy that night in an attempt to find out who was responsible for their son's death. In a deposition, one of the guy's involved said he had driven Andy's truck that night but had not been driving when the accident occurred. In the investigation it appeared that Andy's injuries were consistent with where the Snapchat showed he were sitting in the truck the night the accident happened, with Andy NOT behind the wheel.

In the accident, Andy was thrown from the truck then, for some inexplicable reason, was left in the frozen field for a couple of hours, bleeding internally, while the others took the driver to the ER. Subsequently, "someone" went back to the accident site, in the early morning hours, and Andy was delivered to the ER with injuries then too severe to survive. He lay in a hospital bed for seven days until he was removed from life support and died. His family donated his organs.

When I heard this tragic news, I was overcome with sadness for my friends, and even intimidated by how I could respond to this tremendous suffering and loss. It made me sick, broke my heart for his mom, and even made me feel inadequate at how to face this within our intimate friendship. While this was transpiring, I attended an event where a lovely priest friend gave me a red, glass heart from one of his healing ministries. As the event continued, he randomly gave me a second heart. I knew one heart was for me and when I heard that weekend that Andy's family had donated his heart, I knew the other heart was intended for his mother. I put the heart in my car for when I would see them again in the next few months when they came back to Florida.

One day, awhile later, as I headed into Walmart, I arbitrarily took the beautiful red, glass heart from my car and put it in my pocket. As I walked through the aisles, I heard someone call out my name. Marcus was standing there in the store, having just arrived back in Florida. I hugged Marcus and saw my beautiful friend, Connie, walking up. We wrapped our arms around each other and I slid the red, glass heart into her hand. She took it and there was no need for words in that moment.

Just as the culmination and greatest accomplishment of Christ came on the Cross and through His death, Andy reached the pinnacle of his young life in the gift of his heart, so another man could live. Andy's defining moment was the offering of his heart, through the loss of his life, to another human being, just as Christ's defining moment came from His execution on the cross, in the offering of His life, for the salvation of our souls.

Pope Saint John Paul II says:

> In the messianic program of Christ, which is at the same time the program of *the Kingdom of God*, suffering is present in the world in

> order to release Love, in order to
> give birth to works of Love towards
> neighbor, in order to transform the
> whole of human civilization into a
> 'civilization of Love'." (SD, 30)

This action of love allows us to experience deep love in suffering that we witness. It stirs up compassion and leads us into action. We are meant for action here on this earth to bring this salvific love to others. It is our mission as followers of Christ and in Christ. In our anthropology, the ontological essence of our "being", allows us to imitate Christ, and know our identity in God, and open to the presence of the Holy Spirit. From there we put the Trinitarian love into action.

Also, when we suffer redemptively for others, we raise this love to the highest dimension spiritually. We complete Christ's suffering. Pope Saint John Paul II says:

> ...and all those who suffer have been
> called once and for all to become
> sharers 'in Christ's suffering,' just as
> all have been called to 'complete'
> with their own suffering 'what is
> lacking in Christ's afflictions.' At one
> and the same time Christ has taught

man *to do good by his suffering* and *to do good to those who suffer."* (SD, 30)

In this Christ completely reveals the meaning of our suffering and of suffering redemptively for others.

A friend of mine who's in a Catholic ministry in Michigan posted on Facebook about a year ago that his wife's father, who they had not had a relationship with for a long, long time, was critically ill in the hospital. His wife decided to go and visit him. The prognosis was not good, so they asked for prayers from friends to offer up their suffering for this man's soul. In their time with him, they talked about him receiving confession and coming back into the church. As the relationship was healed, he became open to receiving the sacraments. They called in a priest immediately. This man passed within a couple of hours. On his deathbed, he was able to receive the full healing of his soul and pass into the kingdom of God! This deathbed conversion happened likely because someone over the years – the daughter, his wife, his parents, his grandparents, SOMEONE – chose to suffer redemptively for his soul, and he was converted on the day of his death!

Jesus' obedience put Him on the cross. The love of God the Father, for all humanity, led to the ultimate plan of the sacrifice of His Son on the Cross. Christ takes on all of our sins by taking on suffering. The result of this supernatural event, combining this love and obedience (the Love of God the Father and the obedience of Christ), allows the Holy Spirit to burst forth from this Divine Act, capable of indwelling in all people. This is such a natural, ordered plan of Love that we, in our humanity, participate in it. The love and obedience of a man and a woman to each other in the Sacrament of Marriage and then in the conjugal act, allow a supernatural event to happen where we co-create with God and life bursts forth in the womb as a human baby! This *Order of Love* proves the "truth of that love which the only begotten Son gives to the Father in his obedience." (SD, 18)

Suffering brings forth a potential for a creative element. (SD, 24) We manifest Christ's love as our actions move towards healing as we accept and bear our suffering in union with Christ. In this freedom there is a *completion* in Christ and, that can move us forward. "He Who sat on the throne" declared "I make all things new." (Revelation 21:5) We are made new, in a new embodiment, resurrected with Christ. We create a good that is inexhaustible and infinite.

Suffering can be a tool for creativity and expression. My daughter Dylan is an artist and her creations are often colorful and vibrant and full of joy and life. Yet she has created hallowed paintings that are mournful and expressive. Her art is soulful, whimsical, impassioned, sometimes tragic and complicated. Isn't this a reflection of our journey down the long road...?

Pope Saint John Paull II speaks of "the creative character of suffering" and the good that can flow out from us:"

> For, *whoever suffers in union with Christ*— just as the Apostle Paul bears his 'tribulations' in union with Christ— not only receives from Christ that strength already referred to but also 'completes' by his suffering 'what is lacking in Christ's afflictions.' This evangelical outlook especially highlights the truth *concerning the creative character of suffering."* (SD, 24)

Dr. Sue Ellen Nolan

"The days are surely coming, says the Lord, when I will make a new covenant with the house of Israel and the house of Judah....But this is the covenant that I will make with the house of Israel after those days, says the Lord. I will put my law within them, and I will write it on their hearts, and I will be their God, and they shall be my people."

Jeremiah 31: 31-34

"It is not by sidestepping or fleeing from suffering that we are healed, but rather by our capacity for accepting it, maturing through it and finding meaning through union with Christ, who suffered with infinite love."

Benedict XVI, Spe Salvi 37

Principle Six: Suffering is a Call to Conversion

Pope Saint John Paul II says that in the original Old Covenant suffering is perceived as punishment, "thus in sufferings inflicted by God upon the Chosen People there is included an invitation of his mercy, which corrects in order to lead to conversion...these punishments were designed not to destroy but to discipline our people." This form of punishment is remedial "because it serves to repay the objective evil of the transgression with another evil." (SD, 12) The Old Testament Chosen People of God needed to experience this poverty for God as He consistently led them back to Him. And they were met with His love and His mercy as well, in His invitation to mercy.

Suffering rebuilds the goodness in the subject who suffers. In the New Covenant, which was opened up through Christ and is for all God's people, the Children of the Promise, "with patience await the glory that is to come." (*LG*, 35)

Our Pope goes on to say:

> This is an extremely important aspect of suffering. It is profoundly rooted in the entire Revelation of the Old Man and above all the New Covenant. Suffering must serve for conversion, that is, for the rebuilding of goodness in the subject, who can recognize the divine mercy in this call to repentance. The purpose of penance is to overcome evil, which under different forms lies dormant in man. Its purpose is also to strengthen goodness both in man himself and in his relationship with others and especially with God. (SD, 12)

Suffering can bring us back to God and can bring us back to ourselves. Suffering grows us into spiritual maturity as we remember our need for God, our poverty without God to direct our lives and to form our will to His. The Catechism of the Catholic Church talks about our freedom in these terms:

> By virtue of his soul and his spiritual powers of intellect and will, man is endowed with freedom, an 'outstanding manifestation of the divine image.' By his reason, man

recognizes the voice of God which urges him 'to do what is good and avoid what is evil.' Everyone is obliged to follow this law, which makes itself heard in conscience and is fulfilled in the love of God and of neighbor. Living a moral life bears witness to the dignity of the person. 'Man, enticed by the Evil One, abused his freedom at the very beginning of history.' He succumbed to temptation and did what was evil. He still desires the good, but his nature bears the wound of original sin. He is now inclined to evil and subject to error: Man is divided in himself. As a result, the whole life of men, both individual and social, shows itself to be a struggle, and a dramatic one, between good and evil, between light and darkness. By his Passion, Christ delivered us from Satan and from sin. He merited for us the new life in the Holy Spirit. His grace restores what sin had damaged in us. (CCC, 1705-1708)

Conversion is about a relationship with God. It is in that relationship that we come to know the Paternal love of God the Father. He is our Authority, our Instructor, our firm Father Whose arms we can fall back into. We know that we are loved by Him when we feel the discipline of His love as He teaches us the need for the Goodness that only He possesses. We learn we can surrender to His will for our lives and trust His provision and loving instruction, if we open our hearts to it, if we order our lives to it.

There is victorious power in suffering which "has been singularly present in that victory over the world which has been manifested in the Resurrection" and "He wishes to imbue with the conviction of this power the hearts of those whom He chose." (SD, 25) We can become new persons in suffering, people that endure and persevere and grow in character and hope! Pope Saint John Paul II says:

> The interior maturity and spiritual greatness in suffering are certainly the *result* of a particular *conversion* and cooperation of the grace of the Crucified Redeemer. It is He Himself Who acts at the heart of human sufferings through His Spirit of truth, through the consoling Spirit." (SD, 26)

The Truth of Love Through the Truth of Suffering

Christ transforms us in suffering. That same suffering can transform others when we unite it to Christ's and offer it for their souls.

Redemptive suffering can be used to pray for someone to come into a relationship with God. As we pray and offer our sufferings, we do not necessarily see the results of our prayers. Sometimes it takes years for the miracle of faith and the work of God in someone's life to unfold.

An older church friend of mine told me how years ago she was involved in a ministry, called "Malakai House," a hospice for the homeless and indigent years ago in a major city. The ministry provided a last place for low-income or homeless people to go when they were critically ill and dying so they had a place to seek medical care. She told me of a homeless man who was near death who was given a room to live out his last days. He was immediately grateful for the bed he was provided and wept at the care that he received. He was moved deeply in his soul at the tender care he had stumbled upon at the end of his life. While they ministered to him his heart began to return to God. He asked to see a priest and received the Sacrament of Reconciliation and the Anointing of the Sick. Though his body lay dying, his soul was healed in those last hours. He died in the peace of Christ. Again, someone used their suffering redemptively in prayer for him, somewhere in this world. And his soul was saved! This is the power of redemptive suffering! Father Mike Schmitz puts it simply: "Suffering without Christ is painful; suffering with Christ is redemptive and will transform the world (Illig, Mike, 2016).

A few years back my sister, Brenda, dated a Catholic guy. I was very excited that we might have conversations related to the Catholic Church. One day when we were all hanging out some Catholic hot-button topics came up. I began to see that this guy really held few moral beliefs in line with Catholic teaching. He also seemed to have a bit of a choleric temperament and was somewhat hostile in his responses, which we began to disagree on. The topic of abortion came up and he threw an argument at me that if one of my very young daughters got pregnant, I would take them for an abortion. I had to pause in his questioning and search on how to respond to him. The answer for me became radically clear. It cemented my relationship with the paternal Father, who had consistently taken me by the hand and walked me through many difficult sufferings. It solidified what it meant to have the common term "a personal relationship" with Jesus Christ, the Triune God. And I answered him from my gut. No, I would not get her an abortion. I would do what I have done with all other sufferings: I would turn to my God, my

Father, and invite Him into it. He would answer me and He would show up! He would be the Lord of the book of Job and show His glory and His splendor. No matter what we had to endure, He would be there for me. I know God is real because I have a history and a relationship with Him. This relationship makes it possible for me to go forward with His plan, even amid great suffering. Heroic Virtue means trusting in a God when you *can't see the answer* and you cannot even *conceive of an answer*. He will always make a way for you as God the Father. And He will show up and show you His presence – or that singular grace of Our Lady's presence.

"There for we boast of you among the churches of God for your steadfastness and faith during all your persecutions and the afflictions that you are enduring. This is evidence of the righteous judgment of God, and is intended to make you worthy of the kingdom of God, for which you are also suffering."

Thessalonians 1: 4&5

"Those who pray and suffer, leaving action for others, will not shine here on earth; but what a radiant crown they will wear in the kingdom of life! Blessed be the 'apostolate of suffering!'"

St. Josemaria Escriva

Principle Seven: Suffering Makes Man Worthy of the Kingdom of God

We are led into the revelation of the kingdom through our suffering. Not only do we become one with Christ, but we become one with others. We have solidarity with those who suffer "through the analogy of their situation, the trial of their destiny, or through their need for understanding and care, and above all through the persistent questioning of the meaning of suffering." (SD, 8) Suffering is an invitation to manifest moral greatness! When we suffer, we are immersed in the mystery of Christ's redemption and it makes us spiritually mature enough to desire that our suffering will be used to lead us into the kingdom of heaven. Pope Saint John Paul II says that in a certain way we can repay that immeasurable price of the passion of Christ, which became the price of our redemption, that has been consolidated, made a consistent whole, that is revealed to us in our earthly existence of suffering. (SD, 21) We don't have to pay back Christ for what He has done for us on the Cross, by any means. But we have the ability when we assent to the suffering that is presented to us in our lives and recognize it for what it is: a powerful tool to unite to Christ on the Cross for the redemption of souls. Tertullian beautifully states in, *"On the Resurrection of the Flesh"*:

> "...most blessed, truly, and most glorious, must be the flesh which can repay its Master Christ so vast a debt, and so completely, that the only obligation remaining due to Him is, that it should cease *by death* to owe Him more— all the more bound *even then in gratitude*, because (forever) set free" (Alexander Roberts, Sir James Donaldson T. and T. Clark, 1870, pg. 230).

A year after Regina endured treatment, and during a time of relapse into rebellion, she had been forced to leave my home and move in with her father, who was back in Florida to be near her. I knew I was being presented with the option to participate in the Kingdom of God during the time when Regina was self-destructing and got in trouble with the law. By this time, I had a solid foundation in suffering, even redemptively, and I went to the source of peace that I knew I would need to draw upon. I went to Mass.

I had my "twelve," my support network, I stayed close to God in the Sacraments, and I never went into despair ever again. My suffering had been transformed. I was talking to God personally, with every emotion, sometimes angry and demanding but most often resigned to endure in suffering. I was seeking conformity with God's will and occasionally landing in uniformity, as I was convinced, He was with me at every step.

I was still afraid for Regina and devastated for the path my young girl was floundering on. I sat in the small chapel at St. Cecilia's, oblivious to the people around me and numb from head to toe. I noticed that there was a flyer for an event and I realized it was the *Feast of the Sacred Heart of Jesus* that day. I took comfort in that as I knew Jesus would attend to my hurting heart. As I went to Communion, I received the Eucharist and then turned to the Chalice, I heard the clear, still whisper of a voice from within, asking, **"Will you drink from this cup... with Me?"** It was an invitation from Christ to take up his cup, the cup of suffering, the cup of redemption poured out in His blood, the cup of suffering. It was an invitation to suffer with my Christ! What stood out for me was the words, "With Me". It was an invitation to enter into the kingdom of the Father. Jesus was there with me. Regina's suffering was not over, that journey was still on, but Jesus was with me. Whatever path she was on, it had to be fulfilled. In the Garden of Gethsemane Jesus commanded Peter, "Put your sword into its sheath; shall I not drink the cup that the Father has given me?" (John 18:11)

Our flesh, redeemed in Christ's offering, finds gratitude in the debt that He paid for us as He set us free. We are immersed in this freedom when we unite our suffering to Him. We are participating in the kingdom in our actions when we suffer redemptively, and become an example of living the kingdom boldly on this earth. We become more whole and purer in preparation for the kingdom.

Then eventually *"Christ discloses and reveals the horizons of the kingdom of God*: the horizons of a world...built on the saving power of Love." "Christ leads into this world, into the kingdom of His Father, suffering man, in a certain sense through the very heart of his suffering." (SD,26)

We know, uniquely as Catholics, that we can experience the Kingdom of God here on Earth in the Holy Mass, as well. The Mass is the greatest prayer in the Catholic Church. It is the greatest event on earth!

The Truth of Love Through the Truth of Suffering

In Mass, the kingdom of Heaven unites with the earth in a sacramental celebration of the paschal mystery of Christ. When Christ elevated all of humanity, because of His Divinity, to the divine on the Cross of the redemption He also brought heaven to Earth. We continue this mystery in the sacrifice of the Mass. Heaven comes down on Earth. The veil of time moves away and all the Angels and Saints become present on the altar. This sublime event happens during the prayer of Consecration of the Eucharist. Christ is present, and the Kingdom is present. And we can participate in that Holy Mystery. The Mystery has been opened to us. We experience that beatific vision, and we get to live it, within the Mass!

We also get to live this mystery when we suffer because our suffering was elevated to the divine in Christ. In this mystery we build that kingdom within us. We build that kingdom when we suffer according to His example; and we show compassion when we come together in solidarity with someone who's suffering. We're building that kingdom when we suffer. We're building that kingdom because we're being purified through the things that we experience. We are led into the heart of Christ in suffering and Christ lives in us when we suffer. Christ *lives in the one whom He loved in this way;* He lives in the man" who suffers this way. He lives IN us when we suffer. (SD,

20) The transcendence in this mysterious union makes suffering bearable and brings forth eternal, healing love. This brings us to hope! We can hope in the Cross and in the Resurrection that follows.

Pope Saint John Paul II, writes:

> "To the prospect of the Kingdom of God is linked hope in that glory which has its beginning in the Cross of Christ. The Resurrection revealed this glory — eschatological glory — which in the Cross of Christ, was completely obscured by the immensity of suffering. Those who share in the sufferings of Christ are also called, through their own sufferings, to share in *glory.*" (SD, 22) We can share in the glory and hope even when we suffer, especially when we endure suffering as He reveals His glory to us, in our suffering!

Regina underwent treatment for her eating disorder for three months at Rosewood in Arizona. She came home to me, and we had one amazing year. She was physically gaining weight and muscle. She went back to competitive cheer and we traveled the

South for cheer competitions. She was on the A/B Honor Roll at her middle school. We visited family in Michigan. Our life began to roll out into a happy life. We moved to a new condo to be in the school district she wanted to be in and we had great hopes and great friends, for the next four years unfolding for her.

She began her freshman year on the JV Varsity Cheer team at Riverdale High School with five of her favorite friends. We had sleepovers and cheer parties and though she still used food for control in some ways, she was healing beyond our expectations. Then she secretly went off her medication because she said they made her feel weird and her grades began to drop. She began to spend time with girls that were struggling with grades and school attendance and their families and drugs. Unknown to me she began to smoke pot. She dropped out of all her 9th grade school activities, including cheering at the JV Football games. I found this out from Facebook when I saw her friends were all at their game cheering and she was in her bedroom, door locked and self-destructing.

One day we had a bad argument, that I don't even remember what about, and, when we got home we each retreated to our own bedrooms. After a little while Regina came and knocked on my door, asking if she could use her cell phone. I had taken it away previously because of her behavior during our argument. She wanted to text a friend who had been supportive of her previously, so I gave the phone to her. Regina then retreated again into her bedroom. A few minutes later I received a text from that same girl saying: "You need to check on Regina!" I opened my bedroom door to find Regina standing there, holding an empty bottle of pills which she had just taken.

I immediately called an ambulance and we ended up in the pediatric ICU. I was learning how to endure long-term suffering, but I was terrified and destroyed for my little girl. I wanted her to be okay. I wanted to fix whatever was happening within her. I wanted my girl back.

I woke up, the next morning, in the pediatric ICU on a little green fold-out chair beside her bed, and I screamed out to God. I demanded He show up. I told him that she was just a kid and that He could not let her die – that I needed Him to get involved! I was not pleasant or prayerful. I was angry and I was demanding that God show Himself and do something to heal my kid.

Regina's father, Len, arrived and I went downstairs to call my friend Cathy. On the phone I told her I needed a priest and wanted the big guns. I wanted holy water; I wanted the Sacraments of the Church; I wanted my daughter anointed. Cathy told me there was a chaplain's office there in the hospital and they have priests they can call. I looked up and what did I see but the chaplain sign, right above where I was sitting. So, I walked in and asked for a priest. They told me they would call a priest and, in the meantime, I could speak with the Chaplain. But I didn't want to see the Chaplain. I wanted a priest. I *needed* a priest. I needed the Sacraments and a priest to fight any demonic influence in the evil that had invaded my daughter's life. This was a battle! They told me they'd call the priest and send the chaplain up to me.

I went back up to Regina's room in the PICU and sat there, dejected. I noticed this lady come walking by and sure enough, she's the Chaplain. She greeted me at the door and I followed her down to the other end of the hallway into one of the conference rooms. We began talking but my heart wasn't really in it; I was waiting on the priest. During the course of our conversation it came out that she, the Chaplain, was Catholic.

Suddenly I found myself a little more invested in the conversation, since I felt she would understand my demands. She asked me if I knew anything about Medjugorje. She told me the story of her husband's miraculous conversion, which had happened within the last couple of years, at Medjugorje. I told her Regina's story. The tears began to flow as God broke my heart wide open again. It was beautifully clear to both of us that God had given me His Mother again to remind me that He is real. That He is showing up! And His Mother is there to help me learn to trust Him. As we left the room I silently whispered to myself, "I don't need a priest anymore." And immediately I heard words whispered back, "*The priest is not for you.*"

As we walked down the hallway, I saw two priests walking toward my daughter's room. I knew the older priest, but I didn't know the younger priest, but I recognized his face. I knew the face and the family that it belonged to. Regina had attended Ave Maria Grammar and Prep School for three years with this priest's youngest brother, and had considered him to be one of her best friends. The young man standing before me was the oldest of his family and currently in his first year of the priesthood. They lived in the town of Ave Maria when we lived there and I worked for Ave Maria University. I went to Mass often with his parents and easily recognized his siblings on campus with their strawberry blonde hair and freckles. So, Father Joseph was Jimmy's oldest brother! They looked a lot alike. I knew in my heart that God was showing up again and that when this priest walked through the door of my daughter's room, she was going to recognize his face. I told Father Joseph this, and he agreed, so he walked in the door and he engaged with her. Regina received the sacrament of the anointing of the sick, the sacrament of healing. Yes, God showed up again, He sent Our Lady and He showed up again. I know now, too, that Father Joseph's brother, Jimmy, has answered the call to the priesthood and is in seminary even today!

This discovery (the redemptive suffering of Christ) caused Saint Paul to respond with Love to Christ's love and, "to write particularly strong words in the Letter to the Galatians: "I have been crucified with Christ, it is no longer I who live, but Christ who lives in me: and the life I now live in the flesh I live by faith in the Son of God who loved me and gave himself for me. Faith enables the author of these words to know that love which leads Christ to the Cross. (SD, 20)

Dr. Sue Ellen Nolan

"We are afflicted in every way, but not crushed; perplexed, but not driven to despair; persecuted, but not forsaken; struck down, but not destroyed; always carrying in the body the death of Jesus, so that the life of Jesus may also be manifested in our bodies. For while we live we are always being given up to death for Jesus' sake, so that the life of Jesus may be manifested in our mortal flesh."

2 Corinthians 4:8-11

"In my deepest wound I saw your glory and it astounded me."

St. Augustine

Principle Eight: Redemptive Suffering is a SUPERPOWER

There is a **Supernatural** aspect to our suffering when it is elevated to Christ – in the Obedience of Jesus, and the Love of God the Father – the consummation on the cross unites our suffering to this and invites the supernatural. Suffering clears a way for grace, which transforms human souls. Pope Saint John Paul II says, "The cross was to human eyes Christ's *emptying of Himself,* at the same time it was in the eyes of God *His being lifted up.*" (SD, 22) There is an energy in the cross, the "Word of the Cross" which completes definitive reality the image of the ancient prophecy. (SD, 18)

The Shroud of Turin is purported to be the burial cloth of Jesus Christ. The cloth contains an image, on front and back, that appears to be burned into it. The image is that of a man with markings that seem to correspond to the crucifixion wounds of Christ, from marks on the head, bruises, lacerations across the back, and bloodstains. Pope Saint John Paul II called the shroud "a mirror of the Gospel"(u Catholic, 2020).

Starting in 2011, a team of researchers from the National Agency for New Technologies, Energy and Sustainable Economic Development (ENEA), conducted five years of research on the Shroud. They concluded that they could not replicate the energy that produced the image, nor could they define what type of energy created the image. (Prostak, Sergio, *Sci News*, 2011).

Others have studied the Shroud over the years and have also not been able to definitively say what power source, from ancient history, could exist on earth to burn the image into the cloth. In our Christian tradition, at the moment of the Resurrection Christ came fully back into His body. This would be an event of unprecedented magnitude with powers of the universe that we could not comprehend. A super energy mystery...

"With the Passion of Christ all human suffering has found itself in a new situation"... In the Paschal Mystery, sin and death were redeemed, and "*also human suffering itself has been redeemed*". Pope Saint Paul II writes:

> These are the words of the Apostle Peter in his First Letter: "You know

> that you were ransomed from the futile ways inherited from our fathers, not with perishable things such as silver and gold, but with the precious blood of Christ, like that of a lamb without blemish or spot. (SD, 19)

Suffering was the tool for our Redemption, which raised human suffering to the level of a superpower. The **superpower** of Redemptive Suffering was revealed to me during this crisis in our lives. It was the day before Lent and I was to give a talk on redemptive suffering at a parish in our diocese. In the hospital, after her suicide attempt, Regina had agreed to go to a counseling session and pursue medication to stabilize her. I had renewed hope and optimism that we could get our lives back and she could return home. As we were waiting for the counselor to see us, she became more and more agitated. She knew on some level that she would need to expose herself emotionally when she talked to a counselor, and she was not prepared for that. Out of the deep-seated need for control (which is the nature of the disease) she began to demand that I reward her for going into counseling. I said, adamantly, no. Her demands escalated and soon she was in a full-blown, explosive crisis. The counselor burst into the room to see what was happening with all the noise, and to try and calm her down. She directed me to the other waiting room while she attempted to work with Regina there.

I went to the other waiting room completely wracked with fear and guilt, and feeling destroyed. The talk I was giving at a parish, on redemptive suffering, was from Pope Saint John Paul II's *Salvifici Deloris, On the Christian Meaning of Human Suffering*. Reading, studying, and then teaching it had been part of my lifeline to God and sanity in the chaos during this time in our life. It was changing how I suffered and so, I had to teach it.

I had my notes with me, so I frantically looked through them for some kind of words of peace. There was no one in the waiting room and I was literally up against a wall, in agony, living my Gospel of Suffering. My knees buckled and I slid down the wall as I heard my daughter's cries and agony from the other room. I thought of what God had revealed to me in Job. No matter what was happening, Job never ceased his calling out to the Lord. He railed against God and he expressed intense emotion, but he never stopped asking for the Lord to intervene. His confidence allowed him to demand for the Lord to show up. Jesus, in the Garden of Gethsemane, beseeched God the Father that the cup be taken from Him. And then

He accepted His Father's will. But they both ultimately got a response from God.

So, I was going to call out to God. I told Him in anguish that He was not answering my prayers for my daughter, and that she could die. He needed to step in for her, and He needed to help me find answers to help her. I needed Him to take away the wall that seemed to be blocking any recovery for her. He did respond boldly. He said to me, *"This is her journey. You cannot touch this. You cannot save her from this suffering, but you can offer your suffering to the Cross to save her soul!"* He made it clear to me that I could not touch His plan for my daughter's life. This was His plan and her journey. He would not heal her right then. And He would not take it away. But I, as her mother, could offer my guilt, my pain, my fear, my desperation, my broken heart to the Cross, and He would save her soul.

I could not save her from her suffering in that time, but I could help save her from Definitive Suffering — the loss of her soul — if I united my broken, destroyed, guilt-ridden mother's heart to Jesus' suffering on the Cross. I surrendered my daughter to the Cross and united my suffering to Christ. The only begotten Son was given to humanity to save man against this definitive evil and against this definitive suffering.

The Gospel of Mark tells the story of the paralytic and his friends. Jesus is preaching in Capernaum, and people have heard that He is performing miracles of healing. These guys love their friend so much and want to see an end to his suffering, so they carry him to Jesus, in hope of healing. When they get there it's too crowded to get close to Jesus. They can't get to Him! So, they put him on a mat climb up on the roof. They make a hole in the tiles and lower him through the roof.

When Jesus saw their faith, He said, *"Child, your sins are forgiven you."* The Pharisees call out Jesus for blasphemy against God for saying He can forgive sins. But Jesus knows their thoughts and replies, *"But that you may know that the Son of man has authority on earth to forgive sins."* Next, He said to the man who was paralyzed, *"I say to you, rise, take up your mat and go home."* The man rose, picked up his mat at once, and went away in the sight of everyone. (Mark 2: 10-12)

This Gospel story is about changing our souls. It is about healing our soul. When our sins are forgiven our souls are healed. Jesus wants to heal us from our suffering by healing our souls first. The soul is His priority. Definitive suffering is about the loss of our soul. Christ, Himself, sacrificially has raised human suffering to the level of the Redemption. There is a

The Truth of Love Through the Truth of Suffering

New Covenant accomplished through Christ's suffering in place of us, and therefore, we share in the Redemption. We are also called to share in His suffering that redeemed us.

When my daughter was suffering, and He revealed to me that it was her journey, and that I could not touch it and it would not end, He told me how to use that suffering to save her soul. I was drowning in guilt and shame for my part in her disease. I had divorced her father, moved her back and forth to Michigan, and coped with her problems sometimes by avoiding them, at a total loss. My mother's heart was consumed with failure. But He would not end her suffering, or mine. He offered me the answer by uniting my suffering to the cross and saving her soul. Redemptive suffering is a **Superpower.**

Dr. Sue Ellen Nolan

Pain is part of being human. Anyone who really wanted to get rid of suffering would have to get rid of love before anything else, because there can be no love without suffering, because it always demands an element of self-sacrifice, because, given temperamental differences and the drama of situations, it will always bring with it renunciation and pain.

When we know that the way of love — this exodus, this going out of oneself — is the true way by which man becomes human, then we also understand that suffering is the process through which we mature. Anyone who has inwardly accepted suffering becomes more mature and more understanding of others, becomes more human. Anyone who has consistently avoided suffering does not understand other people; he becomes hard and selfish.

Love itself is a passion, something we endure. In love, I experience first a happiness, a general feeling of happiness. Yet, on the other hand, I am taken out of my comfortable tranquility and have to let myself be reshaped. If we say that suffering is the inner side

The Truth of Love Through the Truth of Suffering

of love, we then also understand why it is so important to learn how to suffer — and why, conversely, the avoidance of suffering renders someone unfit to cope with life. He would be left with an existential emptiness, which could then only be combined with bitterness, with rejection, and no longer with any inner acceptance or progress toward maturity.

POPE BENEDICT EMERITUS XVI

Dr. Sue Ellen Nolan

"But rejoice insofar as you are sharing Christ's suffering, so that you may also be glad and shout for joy when his glory is revealed."
1 Peter 4:13

"For in suffering is contained the greatest of a specific mystery... that constitutes a special support for the powers of Good and open the way to the victory of these salvific powers."
(SD, 27)

The Practical Steps to Suffering Well

During these particularly difficult times of suffering, Jesus revealed to me three practical steps for suffering. These steps give us a means to put into action ways that can assist us when we confront suffering in our lives.

Dr. Sue Ellen Nolan

> "As a body is one though it has many parts, and all the parts of the body, though many are one body, so also Christ."
> 1 Corinthians 12:12

> "As we are taught by divine revelation, penalties follow on sin, inflicted by the divine Holiness and justice...For every sin brings with it a disturbance of the universal order, which God arranged in unspeakable wisdom and infinite love."
> Pope Paul VI (Indulgentiarum doctrina, 59)

The Truth of Love Through the Truth of Suffering

Step One: Gather your Twelve

Jesus had His Twelve with Him on His human journey on this earth. Their personalities and stories put them in different places in the most intense period of His suffering but they were there in all their humanness; and He used them to provide the truth of how, in every story, we could be that person. As in the first principle of suffering, He turned their failures all into good, as the story played out. Regardless of their humanness, they were with Him!

We need our Twelve as well! Gather your people in your suffering. Get your tribe around you, friends and relatives or spouse, a priest or counselor, and the Church. And it doesn't have to be twelve; it could be two or three. Let them know what you are going through. Accept their support and consolation. Have friends that you can text or call at any moment, day or night to encourage you, listen to you, be present to you, or come to you and just hold your hand.

My friend Cathy spent a horrible night with me during the time when my daughter was at her most self-destructive and unstable point. She remained connected to me on the phone and by text as I suffered all through this night. She stayed connected to me through every tear and every sob, every word and every breath. Even if I fell asleep she was there on the phone with me and hanging on to me in my fear and pain. I would doze and she would be there. I would wake and then we would talk a little bit. "Gods still there. I'm still here. I love you. You okay?" Throughout the entire night, she walked me through. She loved me through. I got through.

We need to gather our Twelve when we enter into suffering, even when we're enduring simple everyday suffering. We need to know our team. We need to know our Twelve. That Twelve can be one or three people! We need to know we can count on a text or phone call and we need to have that community. We just have to have someone... We're not meant to do this alone.

Our Lady is one of our Twelve. We have her example as she called her son out into His ministry – even knowing that her own "soul would be pierced." (Luke 2:33) As He walked the road to Golgotha she willed him forward with her Mother's heart breaking. She suffered with Him and yet, with her will united to God, she willed her son to the Cross so His mission could be fulfilled. In the movie *The Passion of the*

Christ, we see her walk that journey with her Son as **she wills Him** to His destination as the Savior of the world. We see her presence. We see her pained glances, her heart blown open in agony, yet she walked the path of the cross with her Son every step of the way. Our Lady is a definitive instrument of the maternal tide of mercy and love that flows through her from God, our Creator above, and she came to me from that mountain to tell me of the birth of my baby girl! Many hearts suffer and an example of how to suffer is revealed not only in Mary's pierced heart, but also (and most importantly) in what her Son, the Messiah who came to redeem us, teaches us in his Passion about how to suffer well. Pope Saint John Paul II writes of Mary, "She truly has a special title to be able to claim that she "completes in her flesh"- as already in her heart- "what is lacking in Christ's afflictions." (SD, 25) Our Lady is there for us too. She will be at the foot of the Cross with us.

One day, a couple years earlier, I was in the confessional at Ave Maria University. It was an incredibly difficult time in my marriage and family life. My eyes were closed as the priest was praying for me and I felt Mary next to me. I felt the imprint of her body in mine. I FELT her against me, leaning into me and me into her. I didn't see her but I felt her bearing me up. She was holding me up in my utter brokenness, and I knew she and I were kneeling together at the foot of the cross.

I knew that Jesus was right above me. I knew He was on the cross right above me. I knew that I could reach my right hand up and I could touch the wounds on His feet. I was compelled to do so and so I reached my hand up to His feet above me as Our Lady held my body up in her strength. I touched the precious wounds of the feet of Christ Jesus. I felt His blood poured out for me. He poured His love out into me.

I told the priest what I had experienced as I cried with gratitude for how much God loved me. He absolved me, in awe as well, and I left the confessional. Though my suffering was still there I was held up again by the love of God in giving me His mother to be with me at the foot of the cross. Afterward, I walked back to my office in the Student Union building. Before I went upstairs I needed a moment and I remembered that there was a little chapel at the end of the hallway that had been used for music storage but was now open. I decided I wanted to go in there for a minute to get myself together. As I opened the huge wooden doors and stepped in, I saw a painting on the wall above the altar, and the sight made me fall to my knees. The painting was of Jesus on the Cross, with Mary, Mary Magdalene, and Saint John kneeling at the foot of the cross. The Cross was just high enough that the three of them could reach up and touch the feet of Christ.

Our Lady is there for us in our suffering. She understands more than anyone. She will bear us up while we reach to touch the feet of Jesus.

Dr. Sue Ellen Nolan

"He loved me and gave himself for me."
Galatians 2:20

"It is hard for us to see in the accidents and trials of life in sickness, in bereavement, In financial loss, in cancerous bodies and leprous limbs, any Divine Purpose. That is why our blessed Lord had to take suffering upon Himself, in order to show us that it is the Father's Cup. Every tear, disappointment and grieved heart is a blank check. If we write our name on it, it is worthless. If we sign it with Christ's name, it is infinite in its value. In prosperity, Christ gives you His gifts; in suffering with faith, He gives you Himself."

Ven. Archbishop Fulton Sheen

Step Two: Do Not Despair

Judas and Peter both betrayed Christ; Jesus knew that they both would betray Him. They both received a look, and a kiss. Peter went out and wept. Judas went out and hanged himself. They both appeared to feel their betrayal and both could choose repentance. Repentance is meant to lead us to contrition for what we have done and to lead us to forgive even ourselves. Did Judas choose self-pity? He obviously chose despair, and despair led to his destruction. Judas' destruction was not in the betrayal of Christ but in falling into despair after it. He lost hope. Peter held on to the mercy of Christ, and therefore didn't despair after his betrayal. We may never know why Judas and Peter made such different choices, but we are allowed to see our humanness in this, and how a lack of hope in Christ's mercy could lead us in such a stark direction. In our humanness we must not fall into despair! God's mercy is never bigger than our sin, or our suffering!

We can be as completely human as we need to be in our suffering; we can become like Job and rail against God. We can call Him out for the bad things happening to us. We can yell at Him, we can demand an appearance, as Job did. Job expressed this in chapter after chapter of him calling on the Lord to make an appearance in the injustice of this paradigm shift of suffering where an innocent man suffers. Even with the prompting of his "friends" and his wife, Job refuses to curse God. He maintains hope on a level that trusts the truth that he knows about God but also allows his humanness on every emotional level. He does not despair in loss of hope.

Jesus, in the garden of Gethsemane, did not despair. He anguished and suffered, He sweated blood in His human physiology. He called out to His Father to take the cup from Him, but in the end He acquiesced to His Father's will. He did not go into despair. He knew His Father had a way to take the cup, but He accepted the cup as His Father's will and plan. He demonstrated to us how to suffer. And in the Resurrection, He showed us there is miraculous glory in the plan of God! Later, in the book of Revelation, we hear these words, "Behold, I make all things new." (Revelations 21:5)

We cannot fall into despair. We must trust the God of hope that there is a plan and a way for us to cooperate. Our redemption came through obedience to a will that was united with God the Father. We must follow the example of obedience even when we suffer in order to allow God our Father the full benefit of working within it. So we are called to suffer, and we can be very human in this suffering. Job gives us his example in railing against God, but we have not left the option to despair. Jesus gives us a clear example of assenting to God's plan and providential will.

In October of 2003, Regina's father, Len, was driving a delivery truck for a local distributor. As he drove down the main road in a busy commercial area a young girl pulled out in front of him, and he wound up T-boning the side of the girl's car with his Mack truck. Witnesses stated that there was no way for him to avoid the collision. Kristen was driving for the first time with her 12-year-old brother, Jacob. Both children were pinned in the car and Len and others were trying to free them as the first responders arrived. One woman was holding Kristen's hand. Jacob lived for 30 mins after arriving at the hospital. Len arrived right after he passed and Jacob's mother fell into his arms.

Although the accident was ruled not to be his fault, Len was devastated, and endured months of intense guilt and heartbreak. Kristen was cited for the accident and Len was required to show up in court for the hearing. In trepidation, we met the family outside the courtroom. Our only consolation was that we had heard they were Christians and had a deep abiding faith, even in this tragedy. Still, there was tremendous anxiety over meeting the family after the death of their young son. The family was there outside the courtroom and we all embraced. Kristen asked to talk to Len privately and told him that she was getting through on her faith. Kristen had been hospitalized with chest injuries. She said inexplicitly that during her time in the hospital the doctors had discovered that she had a form of cancer, which they would never have known about if not for the accident. She said that her brother's life was taken so that she would have the ability to be treated and live. We felt the undeniable presence of the Holy Spirit in this meeting and it worked to assail some of the guilt. It could not, however, take it all away and Len fell into despair.

One day he decided to seek a priest at our parish to deal with the tremendous guilt and grief. He went to Reconciliation. Later he told me that it was a young priest that was visiting our parish. As Len broke down, he told the priest the entire story and admitted that he could not forgive himself for taking this young boy's life. He had never asked the family for forgiveness in the revelation of their strong faith and Kristen's revelation. He wanted to tell Jacob that he was so sorry that he had driven the truck that took his life. Incredibly, the priest shared with him that he had lost his parents in a car accident when he was a very young teen. He had never been able to find a way to tell the person who killed them that he forgave them. In the confessional, they both expressed the words of forgiveness that they needed to say, as the other represented those people involved in these tragedies. Tremendous healing poured from both of them in the acts of divine forgiveness. Grief was turned to an extraordinary resolution of God's providential plan, even in monumental suffering. Despair was turned to wonder.

Dr. Sue Ellen Nolan

"My grace is sufficient for you, for my power is made perfect in weakness."
Corinthians 12:9

"The suffering of this life not only can make our temperament more like the Divine Personality of Jesus, but it detaches us from this world. This Divine preparation opens our souls to the working and pruning of the Father."
Mother Angelica

Step Three: Talk to your Father

As Job railed against God, he kept demanding an answer. He kept communicating with the source of all he knew. When the Lord finally showed up it was not to grant Job's pleadings. It was to show him the majesty and grandeur of Who God is, and prove that He is in control. That Job was not God; God was God, and that was all. He revealed Job's poverty for the need of God to him, and He answered Job by showing him Who He was. This was enough for Job, and he could then endure. God eventually answered his prayers and restored him to all he had before, and more.

In everything beautiful, we can accurately praise God the Father for what He has created. In evil, we tend to turn from Him, blame Him, and even reject Him. God wants our relationship to grow. He wants our relationship with Him. He wants us. We can be completely human in our rantings at God and He can take it. He just wants us to keep talking to Him. He wants us to remember that the resurrection is coming!

As Christ fulfills His mission into a manifestation of glory we can own hope as we wrestle against wickedness that befalls us. *Lumen Gentium* beautifully says about us:

> They conduct themselves as children of the promise, and thus strong in faith and in hope they make the most of the present, and with patience await the glory that is to come. Let them not, then, hide this hope in the depths of their hearts, but even in the program of their secular life let them express it by a continual conversion and by wrestling "against the world-rulers of this darkness, against the spiritual forces of wickedness." (LG, 35)

God, our Father, wants us to keep taking to Him, especially in times of suffering. He wants to draw close to us and prove that He is real. Sometimes in that most intimate relationship He will answer back, in our unique story, and prove it to us!

Christina was raised by a father who never wanted her. She was told this from the time her conception was known. Her father did not want this pregnancy and often said so while Christina was growing in the womb. When she was born she was told she should have been a boy, and she knew her father hadn't wanted her from the start. She was told around age twelve that she was the result of a broken condom.

As Christina came to me for Spiritual Direction we began to wrestle with the disturbing story of her father's lack of acceptance for her from the womb. Though she did feel her father's love as she grew, these feelings of not being wanted and not being loved by her father, became her default feelings when she was at her lowest. As she grew up and eventually married, she developed a relationship with her father but this was always the backdrop. He was sometimes critical and shaming to her and she struggled with self-esteem. One day we decided she should go to Adoration and pour out her wounded heart to God her Father and let Him work in this damaged relationship. She was going to have a conversation with her heavenly Father. She went to a nearby chapel and began to pour her heart and woundedness out to God. In that time it was revealed to her that she was to use all her suffering over the years – from her time in the womb to the present – and give it to Christ, uniting her suffering to His in redemption for her father's soul. The revelation that there would be value in her having suffered for so long buoyed up her spirit.

Providentially, her father began to go deeper into his Catholic faith, which led him to some level of internal healing. Their relationship continued to heal and grow, and they often attended Mass together. Christina and her father were able to discuss some of the difficult things from their relationship, and she began to take back the power to believe in herself. Her relationship with God, as her Father, flourished and fulfilled her. One day when I was reading and praying for her I came upon a scripture passage from Kings: "I have heard your prayer, I have seen your tears; indeed, I will heal you." (2 Kings 20:5) I called her immediately. This divine revelation was conferred on her as a fruit of her assent or agreement to suffer redemptively for her father's soul!

The Truth of Love Through the Truth of Suffering

Dr. Sue Ellen Nolan

"And not only that, but we also boast of our sufferings knowing that suffering produces endurance, and endurance, proven character, and proven character, hope, and hope does not disappoint, because the love of God has been poured out into our hearts through the holy Spirit that has been given to us."
                                                Romans 5:3-5

"God walks into your soul with silent step. God comes to you more than you go to Him. Never will His coming be what you expect, yet never will it disappoint. The more you respond to His gentle pressure, the greater will be your freedom"
                                    Ven. Archbishop Fulton Sheen

The Truth of Love Through the Truth of Suffering: Our Gospel of Suffering

The 1997 movie *Joan of Arc,* starring LeeLee Sobieski, has a very powerful ending. In the story of St. Joan of Arc, she hears heavenly voices that prompt and support her on her life's mission. In the journey toward what would be her martyrdom by burning at the stake, the voices no longer support her. She longs for direction and affirmation in critical times when she seems to be left to her own discretion. At the end of her tragic journey, when she is to be burned at the stake she accedes to her destiny. The only thing she desires is some confirmation that she has not messed this up, that she has not gotten in the way of God. A sign that it has been His will that she has fulfilled and not her own. As she meets her fate, she requests that a staff with the Crucifix be held up at eye level as she is tied to the stake. As the fire begins to grow stronger and engulf her, she focuses on the Crucifix of Christ. The voices return to her in her time of suffering.

God will not abandon us in suffering. He will not leave His children in their time of need. We are not left to wander the desert on our own. It may appear that God is not concerned so much with the suffering we endure. I know I have felt this way many times! In suffering, He leaves us to ourselves in a way that we will seek out our support, our resources, our Church, all purposely so that we will draw close and call out to Him. In the Divine Currency of suffering He is most concerned with our response toward Him. He wants us to draw to Him, not away. He wants us to be His!

God is a God of justice and mercy. If we truly suffered what was due us we would all be in Hell, removed from God and in definitive suffering - the loss of eternal life with God. What does that say about a Father Who does not give us what we actually deserve? Suffering well is a vocation to Love. In suffering, on an ontological level, we become that vocation. WE are transformed at the level of "being!" There is a quote by French author and philosopher Leon Bloy: *"Man has places in his heart which do not yet exist, and into them enters suffering, in order that they may have existence"* (Bourbon Apocalypse, 2017).

With His mercy and love, we journey to the conversion of our heart closer to Him and the reality of our poverty for Him in all things. He wishes us in our suffering to experience the need for Him, and turn to Him. We have all heard the saying that all things happen for a reason. After being seasoned in suffering I can also say, "Things don't always happen for a reason, sometimes things happen and they become reasonable when we bring God into them."

The deepest *need of our heart* in suffering is to find Christ on the Cross. The *imperative of the faith* is to then bring Him into all suffering. We need faith in God – faith that He will come through, through our friends and through our family, through our church and our community. The *need of the heart commands us to overcome fear*, while the imperative of faith provides the context in which to seek out the answer in the right place. (SD, 4)

Suffering is an invitation to mercy, which corrects in order to lead us into conversion. Conversion is overcoming evil while rebuilding the goodness within us; as we recognize this mercy, that is Divine. Our explanations for evil in our lives will be insufficient and inadequate. We must grasp onto the sublime love of God.

Christ walks toward His suffering, knowing His mission as the Lamb of God Who takes away the sin of the world, and knowing the saving power in this act. In His obedience he is united in love to the Father, the same love with which He has loved man. Saint Paul says in Galatians, *"He loved me and gave Himself for me."* (Galatians 2:20)

You will be loved when you suffer! We must be open to that love, when our hearts want to close down. Jesus loves each of us as wide as His arms are open on the Cross! You alone are enough for Him to die for. You alone are enough for Him to suffer for. He wants to come into your suffering, and elevate it. He has taken on our suffering, and therefore He can enter into our suffering with us.

His suffering culminates in the Resurrection, and the power in that is life giving! It is a life-altering power in the greatest act of love. Pope Saint John Paul II writes, "The **'Word of the Cross'** (SD, 18) annihilates evil through suffering. "In the Cross of Christ not only is the Redemption accomplished through suffering, *but also human suffering itself has been redeemed."* (SD, 19) And, *"as children of the promise, and thus strong in faith and in hope they make the most of the present, and with patience await the glory that is to come."* (LG, 35) The evil contained in our own **Gospel of Suffering** can be annihilated with suffering infinitely

The Truth of Love Through the Truth of Suffering

linked to love, rewritten, transformed, and life giving! We can persevere. Suffering is forever linked to love!

I believe my mother is in heaven, and due somewhat to the redemptive suffering she endured here on Earth. For eight years she fought dementia and it took her back in time to an innocent, wonder-filled and child-like final years. She walked her purgatory here on this earth. And then in her last hours she suffered for each of her children.

Incredibly, I believe I have proof that my mother is in heaven. I am the youngest of my family, the last of eight. I spent half of my childhood being the only child at home. My mom and I were like a mother and daughter team. I had the benefit of my mom being financially secure during that time. I was well taken care of and basked in my mom demonstrating her love for me by providing very well for me. Christmas was always magical, filled with love and family and gifts that I needed and gifts that I wanted.

Later in life, because my children were the youngest grandchildren my mom was always a part of our Christmas. She made a point to be with us on Christmas Eve or Christmas Day. When my middle daughter Dylan was born, my best friend gave me a CD of Aaron Neville's Christmas music. One wonderful song was "Please Come Home for Christmas." This song began with the loud *bong* of a bell. We had massive Bose speakers at the time and I began our Christmas morning every year from that point on waking my family with those bells ringing loudly! The children knew Christmas had arrived. My mom was there for countless of these mornings. Many years later, my brother, Bobby, brought a CD to play in my mom's hospital room when we were keeping vigil at the end. The music was from the '50s and '60s and included the original version of "Please Come Home for Christmas" by Charles Brown. Providentially, my beloved mother took her last breath on Earth to this song playing in her room. As my family didn't know of our Christmas tradition, only I felt the impact at that moment.

The tradition has continued. I play that song in my home as soon as I wake on Christmas morning and I send it to any of my kids that are not at home. In those moments my mom comes to me; she is fully present in her spirit. I feel her presence in the eternal love that she is now caught up in, and that eternal love envelops me on every level. I greet her as I am filled with it and she holds me. I cannot describe in human terms what happens but I have had enough glimpses into the world beyond this one to feel what it is. I know only that it is a gift from God each year that continues to reveal to me that He is real and my mom is with Him.

Joseph Pierce is a former Skinhead, who grew up in Britain and lived a life of hatred and violence. He had a major conversion with the writings of G. K. Chesterton while in jail and wrote a book on him. He's now a world-recognized biographer of modern Christian literary figures and an Apologist and professor. He eventually converted to the Catholic Faith. He wrote on suffering in *Solzhenitsyn, Suffering, and the Meaning of Life:*

> If suffering is not accepted it embitters. It twists us. It shrivels us. In contrast, the *acceptance* of such sorrow and suffering is liberating. It sets us free. It allows us to grow into the fully human persons we are meant to be. This is why Solzhenitsyn could bless the prison in which he found himself. He did so because prison had set him free (Pierce, Joseph, 2016).

Often in suffering we cannot comprehend that this could be God working through our lives by His permissive will allowing a suffering. It is sometimes a cruel thought. We do not know the mind of God. We are blinded in the present to anything about His ultimate plan for us. We do not have the ability to have vision beyond the moment, and sometimes, we are not meant to. Our world is often collapsing in on us in these present moments.

It's okay! He is our loving God and Father. He knows and desires the best for us. He is omniscient; He knows the meaning and purpose of every moment in our lives. In her book *One Beautiful Dream,* Jennifer Fulwiler describes the term *wholeness of vision* as being like reading a book to the end, before you can see all the intricacies of all the parts and how they are purposefully played out into a much broader story. It means we are often destined to live in the moment, especially in dramatic suffering, tenaciously in all our humanness, but at the same time, we need to pull into our soul the idea that there is something greater that is happening, something almost beyond ourselves.

One day I woke up thinking about God and my soul. I knew that I needed to go to Confession, but I did not want to go. I had some particular sins I was dealing with and I did not want to go share them out loud. Sometimes it is hard to walk in that confessional door and be vulnerable and exposed. (It always pays off to walk in that door). I began to check out Mass times for that Sunday. Confession would be great, but few parishes offered it before Mass so I thought it would be impossible to pull off. God my Father had other plans.

I was also in need of some spiritual healing, so I wondered about local prayer groups and when they were meeting. I checked one of the parishes that I knew had a prayer group. As I opened up their online bulletin, I noticed that they had Reconciliation before their Mass that day. If I wanted to go to Confession it was available. But, did I want to go? I did not. But it wasn't a hard, solid no... I merely decided I would go to Mass there. It was about a thirty-minute drive, so if I got ready on time and if the drive wasn't too bad then I might make it on time for Confession. I drove to the Church having a conversation with God. Yes, I should go to Confession. No, I did not want to. Maybe there would be enough time. If there was then that was God. I made it to the Church with ten minutes to spare. I looked for the line to Confession. There were a couple of people. If there was time to fit me in that was God. I got in line. A lady stepped out of line and knelt in a pew to pray. The door opened. The door closed. A few minutes went by. The door opened. The door closed. The lady in the pew was technically next. The door opened. She turned to look and told me to go ahead... I'm in.

Turns out I got to be the prodigal daughter that day. Have you been there? I didn't know the Gospel reading was the famous parable of the prodigal son. I had been struggling with going to Confession for a while because sometimes it's so tremendously hard to walk in that door and expose myself and be vulnerable. And today, appropriately, was the perfect day. It was the last confession before Mass started after finding a church that even had Confession before Mass on Sunday. I never even made a conscious decision to go to confession; I just knew I had to go. Nowhere in there did I agree to go in. And it was one of the hardest confessions I've ever made. I had been struggling exceptionally hard with sin. And sometimes they stack up, and I self-destruct. So, then I work them out internally instead of externally; they rumble around inside me and create ugliness and darkness. That's what happened, so I avoided confession for a long time. Can't spend too much time in darkness, right? Or self-destruct for too long, right? I thought I could hit bottom that weekend. But my Lord was ahead of me.

The priest was an awesome young priest whom I didn't know, of which I was glad. I went anonymously behind the screen, which I've only done one other time in my life. After I spat out the words I needed to say, he was short and to the point, compassionate and merciful. And he immediately became Jesus to me. I hadn't cried in a while but I found myself crying there in the confessional. There wasn't much time before Mass began, so the priest said my Act of Contrition would be to sit in the Mass and imagine running like a prodigal daughter into the arms of Jesus. I left the Confessional and knelt in the pew as the opening song began. I closed my eyes and envisioned Jesus in front of me. I, the prodigal daughter, ran to Him and He took me in His arms. The embrace of Jesus healed me soulfully. I felt His presence and a great peace.

But it gets even better, because God is even better. I never realized that the Gospel reading of the prodigal son begins with the parable of the lost sheep. Remember the one that Jesus goes and finds? I knew my Lord had sought me out. In my shame, I ran from Him and was lost. He looked for me. I didn't even want to be found! I did not give full permission to God, when I started my day. I gave confession only a noncommittal shoulder shrug: "If I make it in time, I'll go. If there's not a long line, I'll go. If there is still time, I'll go." Yet, He found me. My heart exploded with joy. "I was lost and now I'm found." (Luke 15:10)

My soul assented when God worked out a way in my life to get me into the confessional and on my knees. I recognized His will for me in how it unfolded, in spite of my lack of cooperation, and since He was so tender to me in bringing me to Him, my heart agreed to wanting only His will for my life! I could not resist His Fatherly way. He knows our humanness and He can work around it. But God is even better than that, because He is God. Kneeling for the *Agnus Dei*, the priest's words filled my soul:

> Lamb of God who takes away the sins of the world, have mercy on me.
>
> Lamb of God who takes away the sins of the world, have mercy on me.
>
> Lamb of God who takes away the sins of the world, grant us peace.

Jesus is the "Lamb of God" Who is innocent and yet, takes on the sin of the world. The Son, who is "consubstantial with the Father." *(The Nicene Creed, 2015)* The Scripture of the Suffering Servant is fulfilled. Again, suffering is linked to love and is redeemed, for us. Pope Saint John Paul II writes:

> The Man of Sorrows of that prophecy is truly that "Lamb of God who takes away the sin of the world." In his suffering, sins are canceled out precisely because he alone as the only-begotten Son could take them upon himself, accept them *with that love for the*

> *Father which overcomes* the evil of every sin; in a certain sense He annihilates this evil in the spiritual space of the relationship between God and humanity, and fills this space with good. (SD, 17)

Dr. Sue Ellen Nolan

"But we have this treasure in earthen vessels, to show that the transcendent power belongs to God and not to us. We are afflicted in every way, but not crushed; perplexed, but not driven to despair; persecuted, but not forsaken; struck down, but not destroyed; always carrying in the body the death of Jesus, so that the life of Jesus may also be manifested in our bodies. For while we live we are always being given up to death for Jesus' sake, so that the life of Jesus may be manifested in our mortal flesh. So death is at work in us, but life in you."

2 Corinthians 4:7-11

"Whatever did not fit in with my plan did lie within the plan of God. I have an ever deeper and firmer belief that nothing is merely an accident when seen in the light of God, that my whole life down to the smallest details has been marked out for me in the plan of Divine Providence and has a completely coherent meaning in God's all-seeing eyes. And so I am beginning to rejoice in the light of glory wherein this meaning will be unveiled to me."

St. Theresa Benedicta of the Cross

~Epilogue~

We sat buckled in our seats on the runway for takeoff from Atlanta to Split, Croatia. The plane glided down the tarmac. There was an other-worldly buzz of energy in the air that permeated every part of the moment. It went directly into our souls. Regina's face radiated excitement, adventure, and joy. Her body was healthy and her mind was healing. I believe she experienced a miracle in healing her body. She was the exception; and no longer struggled with body dysmorphia, thoughts of restricting, or obsessive behaviors. She was maturing into a beautiful, genuine, loving young adult.

So many events had brought us to this place in time. Through so much suffering, Our Lady had come to us. She had brought the mountain to me. Now, she was calling us to her, to come to Medjugorje. Finally, providentially, we were answering her call, and we were going to the mountain.

Bibliography:

Aquinas, Saint Thomas. *The "Summa Theologica" of St. Thomas Aquinas.* Burns, Oates, & Washburne, ltd., London, 1225?-1274.

Archbold, Matthew. 10 Things Obama Might Say to the Pope. *National Catholic Register*, January 21, 2014, 10, pg. 85.

Augustine. *Augustine: Confessions.* Translated by Albert C. Outler, Grand Rapids: Christian Classics Ethereal Library, 1995.

Augustine. *On the Free Choice* of the *Will, On Grace and Free Choice, and other Writings.* Translated by Peter King Cambridge University Press, 2010.

Bennett, D. *The Nicene Creed: Symbol of the Catholic Faith.* 2015. Ancient-future.net. Retrieved on May, 16, 2020, from ancient-future.net.

Bourbon Apocalypse: A Whiskey Son of Sorrow. The Entrance of Suffering.

8 July 2017, *bourbonapocalypse*,
Retrieved on July 21, 2020, from
bourbonapocalypse.com.

Burger, John. George Weigel on Our Turbulent
Times and the Way Forward. *Catholic Digest*,
30 July, 2019.

Retrieved on July 12, 2020, from
www.catholicdigest.com

Catechism of the Catholic Church. New York, NY:
Double Day, 1995.

Chalk, Casey. The 'Dictatorship of Relativism' Has
Arrived. *Crisis Magazine*, 14 Nov. 2020,
Retrieved on July 21, 2020, from
crisismagazine.com.

Coughlin, John J. *Pope John Paul II and* the
Dignity of the Human Being. 27 Harv.
J.L. & Pub. Pol'y 65 (2003-2004).

D' Ambrosio, Marcelino. Blood and Water from
His Side Chrysostom. 4 March, 2018,
Crossroads Initiative, Retrieved on
January 20, 2021, from

crossroadsinitiative.com.

de Liguori, Alphonsus. *Uniformity with God's Will.* Rockford: IL, Tan Books, 1977.

de Lubac, Henri. The Splendor of the *Church.* Ignatius Press, 1999.

Lumen Gentium, Dogmatic Constitution on the Church. Promulgated, Pope Paul VI, on November 21, 1964.

Ek, Phil. "Young Pilgrims." 2003.*Chutes Too Narrow.* Perf. James Mercer, The Shins, Sub Pop Records, CD.

Evangelium Vitae, the Gospel of Life. Promulgated by Pope John Paul II. On March 25, 1995.

Groeschel, Benedict J. CFR. *Arise from Darkness.* San Francisco, Ignatius Press, 1995.

Hallowell, Fr. John. Priest with Brain Tumor Offers His Suffering for Victims of Clergy Sexual Abuse. *Aleteia,* 17 March 2020.

Retrieved on March 22, 2020, from aleteia.org.

Heschmeyer, Joe. Understanding Christ's Humanity and Divinity. *Word on Fire*, 2 May, 2018, Retrieved on March 22, 2020, from Word on Fire.org.

Holt, Lucas. *"The Importance of Both Grief and Joy."* The Cale Clarke Show, Relevant Radio, Green Bay, WI, 15 December 2020, Radio.

Illig, Mike. Feeling the Falls, *The Journey of a Soul*. 6 August 2016, Retrieved on March 22, 2020, from Journey of a soul.me

Joan of Arc. Dir. Christian Duguay. Columbia, 1997. Mini Series Film.

John Paul II. *Fides et Ratio, Faith and Reason*. Pauline Books & Media, 1998.

John Paul II. *Redemptor Hominis The Redeemer of Man*. Pauline Books & Media, 1979.

John Paul II. *Salvifici doloris, On the Christian

Meaning of Human Suffering. Pauline Books & Media, 1984.

Kreeft, Peter. A Refutation of Moral Relativism, *Catholic Culture.* Retrieved on March 22, 2021, from catholicculture.org on.

Kreeft, Peter. Fundamentals of the Faith, San Francisco: Ignatius Press, 1988.

Kubasak, John. Understanding the True Meaning of Freedom with John Paul II, *The Mystical Humanity of Christ*, 5 July 2018. Retrieved on August 1, 2020, from coraevans.com.

Latkovic, Mark. Defining Dehumanization Up, *Catholic World Report*, 26 January 2019. Retrieved on August 29, 2020, from catholicworldreport.com.

Les Misérables. Dir. Glenn Jordan. 1978, Film.

Message of His Holiness, Pope John Paul II, For the Celebration of the World Day of Peace, 1999.

Picón, Jesús. Father Ramos Lost His Sight but Certainly Not His Faith. 4 Dec. 2020, *Aleteia*. Retrieved on January 20, 2020, from theholyrosary.club.

Pierce, Joseph. Solzhenitsyn, Suffering, and the Meaning of Life 13 July 2016, *Chronical Magazine*. Retrieved on July 20, 2020, From intellectualtakeout.org.

Paul VI. *Indulgentiarum doctrina*. Jan. 9, 1967: AAS, 59,5-7.

Prostak, Sergio. Scientists Suggest Turin Shroud Authentic. 21 December 2011, *Sci News*, Retrieved on April 20, 2021, from Sci-News.com.

Roberts, Alexander Donaldson, Sir James T., and Teske, T. Clark R. J. *The writings of Tertullian*, vol. 2, Ante-Nicene Christian Library Edinburg; Scotland, 1870.

u Catholic. *Shroud of Turin to be Displayed*

Online During Holy Week Amid Corona Virus. 6 April 2020. Retrieved on April 21, 2021, from Sci-News.com.

Teske, Robert. *To Know God and the Soul; Essays on the Thought of St Augustine.* Washington, DC: The Catholic University Press. 2008.

Webster's New World College *Dictionary* 4th Ed. Edited by Michael Agnes & David B. Guralnik., IDG Books Worldwide, 2000.

Printed in Great Britain
by Amazon